THE JOURNEY OF A RADICAL YES

[Unleashing Your Adventure]

THE JOURNEY OF A RADICAL YES

[Unleashing Your Adventure]

TABLE OF CONTENTS

INTRODUCTION..1

    WHAT IS YOUR LIFE MESSAGE? 2

CHAPTER 1: FROM THE START 4

    THE PIT OF DARKNESS 9

    INTERNAL HELL 12

    IN A DREAM, IN A NIGHT VISION.......................................14

    AWAKEN MY SOUL 15

    DYING TO THE FLESH 16

CHAPTER 2: THE PURSUIT OF MY HEART 18

    THE FINAL SPLASH 20

    BREAK MY HEART FOR WHAT BREAKS YOURS 20

    UPROOTING 25

    BLIND FAITH 27

CHAPTER 3: PROCESS 33

    RESPONSIBILITY VS. TRUST 34

    SABBATICAL SHEMITTAH 37

    THE LAND OF PLENTY RAIN..39

    TAKING OVER LAND 43

    THE IMPORTANCE OF REST...47

    SEASONS AND KNOWING THE ONE YOU'RE IN 50

    WILDERNESSES AND WHAT TO DO WHEN YOU'RE IN ONE 50

    LOGOS AND RHEMA WORD...56

    DEEPER STILL 59

CHAPTER 4: TRANSFORMING YOUR MIND............64

    FUZZY FEELINGS 64

    THOUGHT LIFE...65

POVERTY MENTALITY..69

WILL THIS EVER CHANGE? 71

COMPARISON IS DEADLY 74

CHAPTER 5: SAYING YES TO JESUS.................76

WHO IS GOD TO YOU? 78

YOUR YES 84

GOOD, BETTER, BEST 85

FINISHING WELL 88

KEY INGREDIENTS 93

CHAPTER 6: COURAGE IS NOT ABSENCE OF FEAR...........101

STEPPING OUT..106

WORDS OF KNOWLEDGE..107

A FIRE IN THE TURISMO BUS 109

AIRPLANE EVANGELISM...112

CHAPTER 7: SPREADING THE KINGDOM 115

PETER'S JOURNEY TO BOLDNESS...............................115

THE MAN ON THE OTHER SIDE OF THE STEEL DOOR 116

NO REASON TO FEAR 120

EVANGELISM 121

OUR DUTY 122

CHAPTER 8: BREAKTHROUGH 124

HOW TO GET BREAKTHROUGH....................................124

TITHING & GENEROSITY 125

SACRIFICIAL GENEROSITY...128

LAYING DOWN YOUR DREAMS FOR A SEASON...........129

PLACING YOUR DREAMS ON THE ALTAR 131

WALKING IN THE REALITY OF A DREAM 133

CHAPTER 9: EVEN THOUGH THE CROPS FAIL............135

DISAPPOINTMENTS 138

DELAYS 142

DEADLINES 144

CIRCUMSTANCES...146

CHAPTER 10: WHO CARES WHAT YOUR LIFE LOOKS LIKE **149**

TRANSITION 149

I HAVE BEEN HERE BEFORE 150

IN THE WAITING ROOM 152

UNLEASHING YOUR ADVENTURE 153

NOTES **161**

INTRODUCTION

Beloved,

It is no coincidence that you picked up this book. I pray that this book gives you the courage to say *yes* to your Jesus. If you are reading this book and do not know Jesus, I pray that you would see, know, and experience how much your Father loves you and that He has always been pursuing your heart. I pray that this book gives you strength when you are weak and faith when you are in doubt. I pray that this book gives you the extra nudge to get out of the boat and walk on water to where Jesus is calling you. This world and all of creation are crying out for you to step into your destiny. Only you can fulfill the destiny that was a thought in God's mind when He created you.

My hope is that this book will inspire, empower, and encourage you to always say *yes* to Jesus and follow Him wherever He goes. I pray that what is possible for me will be possible for you and even greater. That my ceiling would be your floor and for the generations that are to come-that you will take the torch where I left off and continue to run the race marked out for you.

May you step fully into who God created you to be. May you be filled with bravery and have immense courage. May the Kingdom of God spread through your life beyond what you could ever imagine.

WHAT IS YOUR LIFE MESSAGE?

Who do you want to be known as? What kind of legacy do you want to leave behind when you are no longer on this earth? For example, Martin Luther King Jr. had a dream that one day there would be equality for all people, regardless of their skin color. From King's famous speech *I Have a Dream*, King said, "I have a dream that my four little children will one day live in a nation where they will not be judged by the color of their skin but by the content of their character" (source #1). He lived all of his days to see that dream fulfilled. He spoke up and asserted his opinion when it was not well received. He never responded with acts of violence but with peace and conviction.

Now we are walking in the fruit of his life choices where there is equality for all, regardless of skin color. Think about this for a moment: what do you want Heaven to say about your life? What kind of legacy do you want to leave behind?

I want to be known as someone who followed Jesus wherever He went. I want to be known as a woman who took risks and swam upstream when the crowd was swimming downstream. A woman who loved well, spoke up on injustices, spent her life serving others, and equipping others to walk in the fullness of their calling. I want to be known as a woman who accomplished grand escapades with enormous faith, which leads me to my next point.

Faith can become such a common word that it loses its impact without really thinking about the meaning of faith. Faith is defined as: "A strong belief or trust in someone or something. Complete trust or confidence in someone or something" (source #2).

In a day and age where you can ask Siri a question and get

an answer, or Google anything, exercising faith can be more of a challenge. What do you do when you don't have the answer but you feel the nudge to do something that defies logic? What if every logical option is not *the* option? What if God asks you to step out and do something radical without knowing how it will turn out? What if the same stories you read in the Bible are still what God is doing on the earth today?

God wants to write history with you. "God had a dream and wrapped your body around it," said Lou Engle, founder of The Call (source #3). This book was written for you dream chaser; to you who knows there's something more to life.

CHAPTER 1: FROM THE START

One beautiful Carolina day in April, I decided to attend a church I had visited a year prior with a friend of mine. The sun was shining through the pine trees and the Azaleas were in bloom as I walked through the pine needle lain parking lot. Although the season of growth and new life was upon me, I felt like I was internally dying. I was in one of the lowest places I had ever been in my life. I was at a point where I would have done anything to change my life. All the years before I had laughed at church and even mocked those who so faithfully attended. But that particular Sunday, I found myself sitting in the parking lot of a church, hoping that maybe this time church would be the answer.

I walked through the doors of the middle school where church was held and sat in a squeaky fold out chair in the auditorium. That Sunday they had baptism testimonials and every person who shared their testimonies had similar stories to mine. They all came out of a lifestyle of partying, drugs, sex and alcohol and were now completely set free.

I sat in my chair and wept through the entire service. It was as if Jesus Himself was sitting next to me saying, "See Christina, they also went through what you did. Years of brokenness using alcohol, drugs, and sex to numb the pain. I died for them, so they might be set free. I also died for you, so that you would be set free." It clicked that day, like a light bulb switched on when I realized the most profound concept that would forever change my life; *God wants a relationship with me, not a religion.*

To know where I am going, you need to know where I have come from. I was raised in a Christian home where I went to church every Sunday. I would have the same fight with my mother every week about why I had to wear a dress and tights. It would go something like this: "But Mom, these tights are so itchy and this dress is uncomfortable!" My mom would respond, "It's just for a few hours, you'll be okay." I wasn't much of a "girly-girl," I preferred to wear t-shirts, pants, and play in the woods.

The highlight of Sunday school for me was playtime and snacks. I was always relieved to get home and change into my t-shirt and pants and then head out into the woods and play with my friends. I had asked Jesus into my life and had accepted God when I was younger but I didn't have a full understanding of what a relationship with Him looked like. To me it looked like following rules and laws, basically saying no to sins and being a nice polite Christian. I was always a bit of a "rebellious" or strong-willed child. I liked to push the line and adventure. I didn't have the right outlet for my adventurous pioneer-heart, so later in life that led to me turning to the wrong outlets.

My mom was a stay at home mom and laid down her life and career to raise my brother and I. My mom faithfully taught us the basic Christian skills early on in my childhood. She taught us to pray, confess our sins, read our Bibles, and to attend church. She modeled faithfulness beautifully and that is a characteristic of her relationship with Jesus that I have inherited. My mom is a woman who, through the thick and thin, has remained faithful and a devout lover of Jesus. Her faithful tenacity would later prove to be a cornerstone in our lives.

My dad was, and still is, a hard worker. He always provided for us and we were never in lack or need. He demonstrated how diligence, hard work, and responsibility pay off. He always wanted me to succeed and be a successful woman. I'm thankful that my parents taught me these characteristics because I believe they are foundations needed to be a virtuous successful person. They helped lay the bedrock and foundation for the woman I am now.

I loved growing up in the beautiful state of North Carolina. My childhood was full of barefoot adventures in the woods of the lofty pine trees that covered the Piedmont area. I was the child that couldn't be contained indoors but came alive outside building forts, going to the lake, bike riding, fishing and finding animals. I learned about life through the plants and animals that lived in the surrounding woods, creeks, and lakes.

Days spent in those woods would leave me wide-eyed and full of wonder. I would lose track of time as my friends and I ventured into the woods and spent countless hours playing games or building forts. I never wanted to be inside because the outdoor world was a playground for me. In nature, I would encounter a presence that felt calming and yet mysterious. There was so much adventure in the outdoor world, and as a curious child, I was hungry for adventure. My favorite memories of being a child occurred in my own backyard and the woods that surrounded our neighborhood. Now looking back I realize I was encountering the Creator every time I stepped into Creation.

I knew from a young age I was going to do something great with my life. I had great drive and determination to make a difference and see change happen. I always felt deeply impacted by issues that outraged me, some of these included: injustice, racism, and poverty.

The governor of Raleigh wanted to integrate inner city kids with kids from the suburbs. My schools always had a great mix of diversity and race. I hated racist remarks that were made against my fellow classmates and would feel justice rising in my heart. I always had a heart for the kids who were outcasts in school that other children would not pay attention to. I welcomed any new students because I knew first hand what it was like to move to a new school and new state. I always wanted everyone to feel included.

I knew how scary and intimidating it was to start over and leave all of your childhood friends behind. I had moved from Maryland to North Carolina when I was in third grade but that was only the beginning of relocating several times throughout my life. It's important to go back to your childhood and review what made you "come alive" back then. If you get stuck as an adult not knowing what you want to do or what your passions are, your childhood holds a lot of keys for what your future looks like.

My fifth grade teacher Mr. Ferriter was one of the most empowering teachers I ever had. He impacted my life and to this day, he remains etched in my mind because of the values and lessons he taught us. He believed in his students and he demonstrated how we could petition for things from our government and see a change happen. For example, we wrote letters to the school board to fund latticework for our trailer so that our balls and recess equipment wouldn't get stuck under the trailer. The government read our letters and appeals and decided to fund the project and built the latticework under the trailer.

I was amazed by the way he believed in each student. I'll

never forget the day I knew he believed in me. I had always been very performance driven and did well in other subjects but there was one area of school that seemed like a foreign language to me: math. I tested severely low in mathematics and eventually was put into remedial math.

Mr. Ferriter sat me down to go over my report card. I scanned the document for my grades and then stopped, completely shocked, my first "C" in mathematics. I ran out of the room crying because I felt like a failure. It was the first time I had not made an "A" or a "B". Once I had calmed down enough, Mr. Ferriter brought me back in and talked about the ways I could improve the grade but that he was so proud of me regardless. He made sure that I knew my grade was not a reflection of who I was. He never once judged me or punished me for not doing well but rather used that as an opportunity for growth.

Sadly, as I got older I decided it was time to let go of my child-like wonder and stopped playing outdoors and building forts. As I grew into an adolescent and then a teenager my personality became to change and conform to my environment. When I was about to turn 15 my dad sat our family down and told us about a job offer he had been given in Boulder, Colorado. He asked my brother and I if we were on board with moving and shared how much this job meant to him. I felt somewhat excited to start over again in a new place where people didn't know me. I could be anyone I wanted to be. I could re-make myself and start over fresh. I could be the outgoing and lively girl instead of the timid shy girl. Colorado was filled with new possibilities and a fresh slate. At the end of the school year we packed up our house and sold our beautiful home that was nestled amongst the tall pine trees of North Carolina and headed west to the Rockies.

THE PIT OF DARKNESS

Deep down, there was a hurting, lost 15-year-old girl who was searching for someone to validate and affirm her. The teenage years are a crucial point in people's lives where the pressure to conform and fit in is equally as weighty as the strength it takes to stand strong and not conform. Ultimately, I didn't know who I was and the enemy targeted my lack of identity. I wanted someone to tell me they were proud of me, that I was enough, that I was beautiful and that I was made to change the world.

When I arrived in Colorado I decided I was done being the nice, quiet, good-girl. I didn't see the value in maintaining the Christian lifestyle I had grown up with because it seemed boring and uneventful. It felt restraining and seemed unrealistic to live up to the standard that was set in churches. I didn't understand the relationship piece and *that once you say yes to Jesus you are on the adventure of a lifetime.*

The next seven years of my life changed when I met a girl in my Driver's Ed class. She sat in class laughing hysterically as mustard from her Subway sandwich dripped down her shirt. She was high but seemed to be having a lot more fun than I was and I was intrigued. She was adventurous, wild and rebellious. Needless to say, she and I instantly became friends and I began making more friends in the party scene.

I found that being in the party scene allowed me to be loud and unreserved. I became vocal and found that drugs and alcohol gave me courage to be who I really was and that timidity drowned out the more I drank. The things that once held such value in my life like getting good grades, athletics, and my relationship with my parents started to change as I lost interest—I was more interested in partying with my friends.

Even though I was living in one of the most beautiful states surrounded by the Rocky Mountains, I had no desire to be outdoors and explore the beauty Colorado offered. I had no respect for authority and broke any restrictions that were placed over me. I numbed out my feelings with drugs and alcohol. I turned to unhealthy relationships with men for validation. The cycle deepened the more hurt I became in those relationships. My relationship with my parents started declining and all trust was completely broken.

I became extremely angry and put on a "tough girl" exterior so that people would be intimidated by me. I got into several physical altercations and became extremely wild and uncontrollable. I had a deep inner strength that I would not fully understand until later in life but it came out as aggression in physical fights. I thought the tougher my exterior the more people would stay away and not see the sad, lost, hurting girl who was trapped inside. I wanted to be extreme and rebellious and I felt like my life was exciting because I was living on the edge and defying rules.

Under all of that ego and tough exterior was a scared, insecure, teenage girl who was drowning in a culture void of love for the one thing she desired the most; validation in love. I was scared of not mattering, of being too much or not enough, speaking my mind, and letting myself be fully known. The drugs and alcohol would allow me to speak my mind, be free, and not care what others thought.

The deeper I got into drugs and alcohol, the further I was from having a relationship with my family. I was wrecking my life and spiraling downhill quickly. I couldn't hold a job, keep a house, manage money, or relationships. I decided that no one would ever suspect the blonde "preppy" girl to sell drugs so I started selling drugs to support my habit and earn extra money. That came to a quick ending as someone threatened my life and my main source for drugs got shut down.

During those seven years my mom never stopped praying for me. She interceded for me and played K-LOVE, a Christian radio station, in my room when I wasn't there to allow God's presence to fill my room. My parents put down boundaries because the relationship was hurting them and becoming unhealthy. Yet my mom never gave up praying for me. They joined a community called "Tough Love" which is a support group for parents who have troubled teens and helped them stay strong when I was being rebellious. My parents distanced themselves in the context of our relationship. It was too painful for them to communicate with me. They communicated that they were there for me but could no longer have a close relationship with me. I'm thankful that they didn't "helicopter" parent me because it kept them safe and it allowed me to hit my own rock bottom.

To the precious parent, who is reverently praying for your strayed child: never give up hope for them, no matter how many years pass. Continue to pray and believe that the Lord is at work with them. They have a great destiny to fulfill and the devil wants to stop it. There is a war going on for your child and prayer is your God-given weapon. Have others join you in prayer and surround yourself with people who pour into you and keep you strong.

Declare that your child is coming back to the Lord. Use prophetic words and destinies that have been spoken over your child and declare that these words will come forth. If you do not have prophetic words for your child, ask God what He originally designed and created your child for and then declare what He tells you. Use your spiritual eyes to see your child the way God sees him or her. It is easiest to look back at their childhood and take note of what they were good at or gifted with because those are the unique giftings God gave your child to fulfill His plans and purposes.

I also give you permission to not take responsibility for their actions and decisions. The way your child is choosing to live their life says nothing about you as a parent. They are making their own decisions and this is no reflection of your parenting. Just as God gives each one of us a choice to choose Him, the choice His children make is no reflection of Him. Love is giving people the choice to choose. I pray that my story will encourage you to never give up on your child turning back to the Father and that *there is always hope.*

God placed another person in my life who was a complete gift at the time I needed it the most, my manager at Subway. She believed in me even though I was partying, drinking, and coming to work hung over. She saw leadership in me and promoted me to assistant manager before I ever thought I was worthy of such a position. She was a Christian and I believe God used her to start steering me back to Him. This job started to change my outlook on life and I started taking my job seriously. I had decided to stop using drugs at this point but was still extremely broken and drinking a lot. I always wanted to live at the beach and decided I was going to make a drastic change in my life.

INTERNAL HELL

You can change locations but that still doesn't fix the problem. When I turned 21 I decided to move back to North Carolina for a fresh start once again. I was living at home and saved up as much money as I could and then packed my Honda Accord full of boxes and all of my items. My mom and I drove across the U.S. from Colorado to Wilmington, North Carolina. I enrolled in a few classes at the local community college to see if college was something for me or not. Prior to enrolling, I had no desire to attend college. I was slowly starting to regain confidence in myself that I would actually become successful and make something of my life.

Once I stopped using drugs and smoking marijuana every day, my anxiety and panic attacks became extremely severe. My nights were filled with drinking to numb the anxiety and panic. I came to a point where I was unable to function and was heavily medicated on Klonopin and Effexor. I couldn't be in a room without knowing where the exit was in case I needed to make a quick exit. I couldn't ride in cars if I wasn't driving in case I needed to pull over and get out. Any situation that I felt trapped and claustrophobic would bring on a panic attack.

I was sitting in science class at one of the black lab tables as I looked up at the clock. *Another hour and half, how am I going to make it through this class?* My brain started running and soon I noticed my breathing was becoming abnormal. *I need to get out of here but I don't want everyone to look at me. I'll just quickly grab my bags and quietly walk out. I have to get out of here.* Once I hit the elevator, in a full blown panic attack, I wanted to turn to the girl that was next to me to and scream, "Help! I'm dying call an ambulance!" The elevator started becoming a tunnel as my sight narrowed. I thought I was going to die or pass out.

As soon as I got off the elevator I ran outside and lit a cigarette and took a few puffs but that didn't seem to help the problem so I smashed the cigarette under my foot and kept walking. I walked down the hill to my car once I got inside I cried and screamed, "I'm losing my mind! I can't sit in class anymore! I can't go anywhere because I'm afraid I'll have another panic attack and embarrass myself! I'm going crazy!"

My life was literally a living hell. This happened multiple times a day for over a year. I was locked in the internal prison of my mind and it seemed like no one had a key that would let me out. I would drink to the point that I couldn't feel these awful anxious feelings only to fall into the same cycle the following day. I felt like I was trapped, going crazy, and going to die.

There was nothing anyone could do to help me because the war was inside my mind. I remember being very concerned for my own life and well-being at that point but I didn't know how to stop it. If I didn't drink the panic attacks away, they would keep coming but the drinking only seemed to exacerbate the problem. I knew I was spiraling downhill at a fast rate but I didn't know how to break the cycle. While all of this was going on I started having a repeating dream.

IN A DREAM, IN A NIGHT VISION

The world was ending and the earth was covered in complete darkness. There was no electricity, and neither the sun nor moon was shining. I was watching as a war was going on around me on earth but I didn't know where I was going. People were running and screaming in complete chaos. It looked like a war scene, except it was completely dark. As I looked around I began to see people being lifted to Heaven. A woman came up and would ask me, "Do you know where you're going?" I said, "No, I don't know." Then she said, "It's your turn to talk to Him."

I was lifted before the presence and throne of God and I felt overwhelming light and peace. He looked at the book of life and said, "I don't know you." I started to beg and plead with

God saying, "Yes, you do know me, I always knew this was the way, I just couldn't get my life together." God responded, "I don't know you, you chose to go down the other path." At that moment I was back on the earth surrounded by utter darkness watching souls being lifted to Heaven and thinking, *I missed my chance.* This dream not only came more and more frequently but I would wake up wondering, *if I were to die today, where would I go?*

AWAKEN MY SOUL

After months of having this repeated dream and cycling through anxiety and panic attacks I decided I wanted to go back to church. I felt a pull deep inside me to see if God could be the answer in breaking the torment I was experiencing. That Sunday I went back to church my life forever changed. I accepted the Lord sometime within the following months and started walking with Him again.

It wasn't easy because I was still living with one foot in the world and one foot in the church. I would live one way during the week and then another way on Sunday mornings. I was trying to cling to my old lifestyle because I was too afraid of completely letting go. It never sat right with me but I didn't know how to change because the life that was slowly slipping away from me was all I had known those last seven years.

This is the beauty of God. Every single person can come to Him just as they are. No matter how much you have messed up, how low or inadequate you may feel, or how many times you have fallen, God's arms are always open to you. You are always welcome to come back home to Him. He specializes in taking people out of the pit, cleaning them off, and breathing life into them again.

I was often hung over and riddled with anxiety as I sat through church but He welcomed me with open arms. People will not come into the Kingdom cleaned up based on their own doing; hardly ever do you see in the Bible that Jesus went after those who were clean. He went to those who were sick and sitting in sin. Through knowing Him they became clean. Jesus said, "It is not the healthy who need a doctor, but the sick" (Luke 5:31). We must have our arms open to the lost and hurting and take them in just as they are, not when they are fixed up.

DYING TO THE FLESH

The final straw for me was when we threw my friend a birthday party. It was around noon when we started the party but by 6:00pm I had lost all recollection of what had happened. That was the first time in all of my drinking days that I blacked out.

When I woke up the following morning, the house looked like the aftermath of a hurricane. Glass was broken and shattered everywhere, the bookshelf was turned out from the wall, and there were cups and paper plates everywhere. I woke up one of my friends on the couch and asked her what had happened. She said I had went crazy last night and caused all the damage and kept dropping and breaking glasses. I was shocked that I was capable of causing that much destruction and not remembering any of it.

As I tried to regain recollection of what had happened I felt like I was dying. Not only from the hangover but also because I knew I couldn't live like that anymore. I couldn't live life with one foot in the party scene and one foot with Jesus.

For the first time in seven years that lifestyle no longer sat right with my soul. This time something was different. The still small voice of the Holy Spirit that I had drowned out all of those years was convicting my soul and reawakening a conviction to come into complete righteousness and holiness. I was devastated that I had once again "messed up" and wasn't strong enough to say "no" to my old lifestyle. I felt covered in shame and slimed with guilt. The devil was pointing his finger at me laughing and telling me that I would never change. I remember thinking, *"I can't live like this anymore but how can I ever change?"*

Words do not express the feelings that I felt that day. Part of me felt so hopeless that I would never changed, while part of me knew I had no other option. I tried to change on my own the months prior and I was utterly failing. Part of me was scared that I would make this commitment to God but not be able to live up to it. I was too weak to change myself. But thank God for Jesus because He came to make us strong in our weaknesses.

I was scared to completely let go of my friends, my old life, my old habits, and allow God to completely come into my life. At the same time I was tired of living so recklessly for the last seven years. It wasn't fun anymore. It came with a cost and it had cost me a lot of hurt, pain, wasted money, sickness, and destruction.

I turned to God and cried, *"God, I'm such a mess. I don't know how to clean myself up or change this. I can't do this on my own. I don't know how to even begin or how you can change me, but I need your help."* I knew I could not continue living like this and I couldn't change my life on my own. I needed Jesus; I needed a redeemer and a Savior. I needed help.

CHAPTER 2: THE PURSUIT OF MY HEART

From that night on I made some major changes. I quit going to the bar and in replace of that I had a friend who I would go fishing with on the weekends. We would fish at the beach every Friday and Saturday night to occupy our time. I told myself I could no longer go to clubs, be at the bar, or go to parties. I had to set really strict boundaries for myself. I eventually even had to move out of the house I was living in to live with someone who would hold me accountable for my new life. It wasn't easy at all and I got mocked and ridiculed a lot for the sudden change. I was in a learning process and sometimes I fell, but Jesus was there to walk me through every step of the way. It was a gradual change but from the moment of my darkest point and total surrender, my life began to slowly climb out of the pit.

I can see Him now, smiling at me even though I looked at Him through the lens of shame. I stood before Him completely covered in dirt, slime, and muck. With those loving eyes and that smile, He joyfully cleaned me off. He put a new heart in me. He exchanged my dirty clothes for pure white ones; He healed me and set me free. His daughter had finally come back home and He couldn't be more proud. There was a burning desire in me to completely be changed as I set my eyes on my beautiful Savior. It takes time to renew poor thinking patterns and lifestyles but I never quit. I had an unquenchable hunger deep within me.

I started going to a small group where the women loved me for who I was. They never once judged me but loved me through my process. I moved in with a friend who demonstrated the secret place with the Lord beautifully. Most mornings while I made coffee, my friend sat at the kitchen table with her Bible and a notebook open in front of her. Nothing—not even my presence in the kitchen—seemed to rattle her attention to those words that, until now, seemed so dead to me. Seeing her hunger for the Lord made me desperate to experience it for myself.

My friend's secret place with the Lord was contagious. I began to develop a devotional life with the Lord from that place. I was hungry to seek Him every morning, to pray, get in the Word and journal. The words of the Bible sank deep into my spirit, like seeds, and began to grow. I devoured books and devotionals with ravenous hunger. I broke off every soul-tie I had to any man. Breaking off soul-ties means that you forgive the person and yourself for the broken relationship and you release and bless them. As I forgave them, I found more healing for myself.

Everything was beginning to change, but it was not without effort. I had to put my hand to the plow and grasp the handles without letting go and push ahead. I was turning up the dirt and deep-rooted destructive patterns in my life. I had to till the land with the Holy Spirit as we dug up old thinking patterns and uprooted weeds that had grown deep roots into my thinking patterns. I had to believe that my life would actually change even when it felt like it would take forever. Like a candle in a jar full of holes, I was beginning to get glimpses of freedom from this journey I had started on.

THE FINAL SPLASH

A few months later I knew I wanted to be baptized as a symbol that my old life was gone and that I was putting on my new life. That Sunday I sat in my car riddled with fear and kept thinking: *people know me in this town and there are people here today who know my past and my history. I can't get up there in front of thousands of people and do this. What if I mess up again?* I called my mom and she said, "You get up there and get baptized! That's the devil lying to you to keep you from doing it." I got out of my car, full of jittery nerves, sweaty palms, and a dry mouth and I walked into the sanctuary to be baptized. In September of 2008 I shared my testimony and made a public declaration at Port City Community Church in Wilmington, North Carolina and was baptized.

BREAK MY HEART FOR WHAT BREAKS YOURS

A few months later, my friend and I strongly sensed that we were to go on a mission trip. One Sunday I made my way over to the missions table and began looking at countries and pictures. As I scanned the table, my eyes stopped on a picture of a group of Mayan women dressed in vibrant colorful tribal clothes. My heart felt like it was being pulled into the picture. In that instant I knew this was the trip I had to go on. I couldn't even pronounce the name of this small rural mountain town located in between the vast green mountains of Guatemala. Sadly, I didn't know where Guatemala was located because the geographical nations were never on my radar. I signed up for the trip to Chichicastenango, Guatemala with no idea of what was in store for me. That trip would later prove to be a pivotal part of my life.

When I sat down to write my support letter I could feel the

tangible presence of God all over me. It felt as if God had His hands on my shoulders, like an all-encompassing blanket of peace that was helping me write the letter. I knew with certainty I would be going on this trip. It was a huge step for me because it was the first time I had asked for money for a mission trip. Of course, all of the money quickly came through and I was soon on a plane to Guatemala.

The plane landed in Guatemala City and instantly the smell of wood burning stoves and exhaust filled my nose. I breathed in the humid air and began taking it all in. The city was busy and full of activity. Food, markets, people, colors, and culture were everywhere. My eyes could barely take in everything as we drove around the city. I felt like a little kid on Christmas morning, I was filled with so much excitement. There seemed to be no driving laws as our team made our way around the city in a large bus.

After a few hours of sitting in traffic we began to make our way into the majestic mountains of Guatemala. The clouds hovered over the mountains as we drove in and out of fog. We drove by some of the highest mountains I had ever seen accompanied with volcanoes. The land was rich and vibrant with color. People were working in the cornfields as women were walking on the side of the road with babies wrapped in beautiful linen on their backs. The men working in the field would stop plowing as they looked up to see a bus full of "gringos." I had never seen such a beautiful country. It held an enchanting beauty unlike anything I had ever seen or experienced before.

As we came into Chichicastenango, the streets thinned and the smell of wood burning stoves intensified. Chichi was bustling with people and movement. As I looked around I could feel the spiritual heaviness for the town. It was very poor, grey, and run down. Drunk men laid out on the sidewalks and streets. Smoke filled the air from the incense that was burned on the front steps of the church. Amidst all the grey colors of the buildings the heaviness that I could feel in the air, there was joy.

The market place buzzed with people and the unique colors that were woven into the women's tops and skirts added a rich vibrancy to the atmosphere. The people were filled with joy and the children were always smiling. Their smiles warmed my heart and, little did I know, would change my life forever. *People who had so little yet had so much happiness.*

Guatemala awakened my heart to what was going on outside of my safe, comfortable bubble in America. I had never been outside of the country before and the way people lived was shocking to my first-world mindset. I began to understand just how fortunate I was growing up where I had. One night our team was gathered around a fire to pray. While we started praying, the fire burned down to embers. I prayed a simple prayer inside my head, "God, break my heart for what breaks yours." Within a few minutes the entire fireplace was engulfed in a large flame. It was so loud all of us stopped praying and stared at a blazing fire in the fireplace, where just moments before there was nothing but embers.

In that moment, I realized another side of God's face, the power of a supernatural God. His presence became visible through the fire. He took our prayers like a burnt offering and He would surely fulfill what we had asked for.

The next morning we headed out to the school down the street. While our team was handing out vitamins to the children at a local school I felt incredibly overwhelmed with love for the kids, the people, and everything I had seen that week. As I looked around the room at the beautiful coffee colored children with their bright brown eyes and white smiles, I began uncontrollably crying. I stepped outside the school to try and gather myself but nothing would stop the intense pain of the heartbreak I was feeling.

One of my missionary friends who lived in Guatemala asked me what was happening. She said, "What did you pray for last night?" I remembered, "I prayed that God would break my heart for what breaks His." "Well, it seems to me He answered your prayer; be careful what you pray for," she said with a smile and suggested I go talk to God for a bit. I walked up to the top of one of the lush green mountains that overlooked the town of Chichicastenango.

As I walked up a dirt trail where many generations had walked before me I found a spot that overlooked the town. I asked God, "What are you doing in me?" He replied, "Christina, I'm showing you a glimpse of how my heart breaks for my people. This is just one place on the entire planet of where my heart breaks. You couldn't handle all of it. This is just a glimpse of the same feeling I had when I watched my Son die on the cross that day."

I sat and cried on the mountain that day. I struggled to be with the group as they went to the orphanage because I was so incredibly wrecked by what had just happened. I sat in our team's bedroom full of bunk beds and tried to eat a peanut butter and jelly sandwich through non-stop tears. I was so radically changed by that encounter and the compassion God has for His people. That day I was marked with compassion and would never be the same. A seed had been planted inside my heart that would only continue to grow deeper in the years to come. Why would God not want to give you more of His heart? Would you dare to pray this risky prayer right now? *"God, break my heart for what breaks yours."*

If what I experienced that day was only a glimpse of His compassion, I can only imagine the kind of experience I would have if I encountered the fullness of His compassion. I actually don't believe my mortal body would be able to contain it. The night we got back to the Raleigh-Durham airport I sat on the bus and whispered, "God, I will give you my house, my car, my dog, my life. I will give you everything. If you will send me, I will go." In that moment I was crying out to the Lord and His eyes were searching the earth, like it says in 2 Chronicles 16:9 (NLT), "The eyes of the Lord search the whole earth in order to strengthen those whose hearts are fully committed to him." The answer to that is found in Isaiah 6:8 (NIV), "Then I heard the voice of the Lord saying, 'Whom should I send as a messenger to this people? Who will go for us?' And I said, 'Here am I. Send me!'"

If I could sum up what happened in 2009, it would be exactly that: God's eyes were searching the earth and I was saying, *"Here I am. Send me!"* God wants to do the same for you. He is searching for a people who will say *yes* and rise up to follow His purposes on this earth. He is searching for the ones who will surrender their heart and give their life fully to Him. Allow God to take you where He needs to so that your heart can be broken for Him. Allow Him to fill you with compassion and that like Jesus, you would be led forth and moved by compassion.

The years that followed that prayer took me on a wild adventure with my Jesus. God had asked me to surrender everything that I was holding onto and to be completely sold out for Him. Every area of my life that provided a false sense of comfort was stripped from me as He invaded those areas and replaced them with firm founding security. I remember walking my dog one day and I knew the day was here; I needed to find her a new home. I had a "knowing" in my gut that I was about to be moving and traveling and I wouldn't be able to have a dog. As someone loyal and determined who doesn't give up, I struggled with re-homing my dog because I felt like I was failing her.

I loved her like she was my own child, I picked her up when she was 14 weeks old and she sat on my lap as we drove to my house. She was there through the darkest of nights and she was there when I found Jesus. At the time I got her, I really needed something to take care of. Having a dog brought so much joy to my life and it held me accountable when I was transitioning out of my old lifestyle. I told the Lord I would only give her away if He found the perfect family for her and gave me peace about it. I had several responses to the ad but never felt peace about the people who were interested in taking her.

One afternoon, while the sunrays beamed through the Carolina pine trees, I pulled up to meet the 3rd family who was coming to meet her. Before they even rounded the corner I began crying. I knew this was the family who would take her before they even said a word. I prayed that she would bless them beyond how she had blessed me. Sure enough they were the ones who re-homed my dog and several months later they said she brought the dad out of depression and had been a huge blessing to the family. I grieved her for close to a year as I was also going through one of the most challenging seasons I have had yet. As the months progressed I sensed my time in Wilmington was coming to a close.

UPROOTING

Prior to me leaving Wilmington, North Carolina I got a

directional word from a friend the following morning. Over a cup of coffee she told me, "The Lord is getting ready to uproot you. I don't know where He is moving you but get ready to move." That word confirmed what I had been feeling in my Spirit. I felt unsettled and that I needed to have myself in a place where I could be ready "to go" at any moment but I didn't know where I was going. Her word confirmed why I was feeling like I was being uprooted. It wasn't until eight months later that her word came to pass.

It doesn't have to make sense to us, to see life as God sees it. So often, what He asks of us doesn't make logical sense. Being uprooted can be one of the most painful processes. Everything you know, your community, your comfort, all of it is slowly stripped away until you are left with just you and Jesus. Let Him woo you to follow Him into the unknown and leave behind everything you once knew.

Just like the disciples left behind everything they knew to follow Jesus they were confronted with a question when the road got narrow. Many of Jesus' disciples had just left when He turns to His 12 and asks, "Do you also want to leave?" Peter replies, "Master, to whom would we go? You have the words of real life, eternal life. We've already committed ourselves, confident that you are the Holy One of God" (John 6:67-69 The Message Translation). His disciples had left behind their previous lives and encountered the One, who had eternal life, so what would they have to go back to?

In this day and age there are so many comforts and distractions it is easy to hold onto retirement, 401k plans, job security, and relationships instead of the only true security, which is Jesus. The Father was inviting me on a journey to come and know Him deeper. If I would just let go, He had a vast ocean of promises that were ahead of me. I often see the popular meme of a little girl wanting to hold onto her small teddy bear and Jesus is down on one knee asking for the small teddy bear so He can give her a much larger one that He is hiding behind His back in His other hand.

Whenever He asks you to give something up, it is because He has something much greater coming in return. Make room for the "more" of what God is doing. Relinquish control and be wowed at the ways He comes through for you and the places He will take you.

Stepping into the unknown is not comfortable because you are navigating through an area you have never been before. I knew I was supposed to leave North Carolina and follow Jesus to Oklahoma but I had no idea why. It didn't make sense to leave everything I knew and had spent years building up. I had no job opening, just a deep sense within my spirit that Oklahoma was calling my name.

BLIND FAITH

When I said *yes* to, "Send me, I will go," I had no idea what I was in for. Moving to Oklahoma, I had blind faith—no idea what my time would be like. I prayed that I would find a church that was fully going after more of God and the Holy Spirit. I was challenged by the words of Jesus in John 14:12; "Very truly I tell you, whoever believes in me will do the works I have been doing, and they will do even greater things than these, because I am going to the Father." I wasn't seeing the greater works of Jesus let alone the works He had been doing. I knew there was more and my hunger led me into a wild adventure.

I would doubt myself when I was first learning to hear from God. I went back and forth between what God said and what made logical sense. I was going through a process of uprooting fear, lies, and strongholds in my mind, and I wasn't confident in my ability to hear God's voice. For example, I got to the point where I was feeling so unsettled that if I didn't make a decision to move I would have been directly disobedient. I kept going back and forth to stay in North Carolina or go to Oklahoma. The decision that made the least sense was the one I had the most peace about. I had a really hard time coming to a decision and kept asking God to make it clear to me.

I was on my lunch break from work and was sitting in my car when I heard so loud and clear it was almost audible but I heard God speak to my spirit: "Move to Oklahoma. This is your next assignment. I'm going to use this time to knit your family back together and for you to get out of debt."

When I told people I was moving to Oklahoma, many people didn't understand why I would go or what was out there for me and the honest truth was neither did I. But I had peace even though I couldn't see what was ahead of me. I learned in previous seasons to always trust your peace and move in that direction even when it didn't make sense. Brick by brick I was beginning to build a foundation of trust with the Lord.

My time in North Carolina was like a dream but suddenly the mirage of everything I thought I wanted wasn't the direction I was beginning to move in. All I wanted was to live at the beach, have a boat, a nice family, and open a women's rehab home. That's not a bad dream; it just wasn't God's dream for me.

I packed my little Nissan and drove with a treasured friend of mine all the way to Oklahoma. As we hit every state line from North Carolina to Oklahoma I would cry as the reality of what I was leaving behind set in. I had no idea what was ahead and quite frankly, the unknown scared me. I was actually doing it, following God's voice in blind faith. Once I arrived in Oklahoma I started applying to jobs and had several interviews but could tell I hadn't landed on the right job yet. Then, I was interviewed for a position that I was under qualified for. Technically, I needed a master's degree to run the women's rehab but I found favor with my boss and my experience and bachelor's degree was enough.

From there I paid off my remaining credit card debt. At one point I was $10,000 in credit card debt from living an out of control lifestyle. I was constantly being challenged at my new job as I maneuvered through being in charge of up to 50 women and managing an entire rehab facility. I was in over my head the entire time I worked there. This wasn't the first time I felt this way either, my first two jobs post college were "over my head." God showed me how much more He could do with me saying *yes* to Him, than feeling qualified for a job. He was the one who enabled and qualified me.

My time in Oklahoma was so valuable to me. It was stretching and challenging as I grew in my role at work. I encountered God in an even deeper way and got involved in a wonderful church in Norman, Oklahoma that is part of the Antioch Community Church movement. In this church I experienced the prophetic ministry, gifts of the Spirit, healing, and the more of what Jesus was talking about in His gospels. I knew my time in Oklahoma was short, but through my church I learned that we still hear God's voice, He still heals, and that the prophetic is meant to encourage and uplift us. Being in Oklahoma was imperative to my next step.

Once my credit card debt was paid off I felt released to leave my job and start on my next adventure, which was a five-month commitment to a ministry in Guatemala. At the ministry I worked on a discipleship team with two other local employees. We would drive through the windy roads in the mountains and hike to different families' that lived in the Quiche area. When I wasn't visiting families I helped with some of the feeding programs for children and missions teams that came to help the ministry.

Living in Guatemala was really one of the most beautiful times of my life. I was beginning to learn how to trust the Lord with my finances as I began fundraising. I was again in "over my head" as I was moving to a country where I barely spoke the language and a town that spoke a different dialect. Once I arrived there I had more downtime than I imagined I'd have. I lived in the very small rural mountain town of Chichicastenango, Guatemala, so there was not much to do there.

Oftentimes the power or wifi would go out and I had to re-learn how to function without my usual go-to. I started painting again, writing, spending hours in worship, enjoying the outdoors, and exploring the culture and town I lived in. While I was in Guatemala, my favorite past time was spending hours in worship and prayer communing with my Father in the rural mountains of Chichicastenango. This was an imperative part of my life because I had to learn to be content being with my Father and not doing anything for Him to feel significant.

I sat up in the prayer chapel that overlooked the city of Chichicastenango and breathed in the fresh air laden with rain and the smell of wood burning stoves. The foggy clouds engulfed the mountain and the rain poured down. I didn't care how long I was up there; I just wanted to be with my Father. I didn't have the restraints of time or the hustle and bustle that goes on in the United States. It was still, quiet, and calm and I could hear God's voice every day because I created the space to do so.

My heart was changed by the way the Guatemalan people loved me and were so generous when they had nothing. They had joy in the midst of their circumstances. I realized happiness was not found in materials, like I once thought it was, but it was found in the presence of God. The very things I had thought would make me happy were facets of real joy. Real joy is not dependent on circumstances or things. I still reminisce about this time and how I was literally on a honeymoon with my Creator. Some days were very hard because I did feel lonely and I wanted to go home but other days I knew I was exactly where I was suppose to be.

Amidst such beauty and wonder I could feel the tangible spiritual heaviness of Chichicastenango every time we would enter into the city. There was a sense of hopelessness that could be seen even more on a cloudy dreary day. I was still battling fear over the darkness and witch craft that I saw going on. I knew I was called to change Guatemala but I knew I was lacking the tools to complete the task ahead of me. I had so much fear about darkness and demons. I didn't understand at the time the fullness of the authority I carried.

After completing my term in Guatemala, I knew the Lord was calling me back to United States to get equipped. I headed back to Oklahoma unsure of what lied ahead. When there is a dense fog that sits over the next step of your life and you can only see one foot in front of you, the Father is calling you to trust Him with the unknown. We don't know why He calls us certain places but He is always setting us up for the best possible outcome. He takes us through a journey, equipping us a long the way to fulfill our calling.

Once I moved back to Oklahoma I got a job working as a disaster case manager for the Oklahoma Disaster Recovery

Project that focused on helping victims from the tornado that destroyed Moore, OK on May 5th, 2013. I really enjoyed working for the project and speaking at funding committees on behalf of the people who lost their livelihood in the tornado. I knew I wasn't staying in Oklahoma long, but I stayed there until I got clarity. Bethel School of Supernatural Ministry in Redding, California kept coming up and the more I looked into the school, I knew God was calling me to go there.

The next few months I saved up enough money for my next big move to California. It made no sense to me to move out to California where I knew no one and had to start all over again. But at the same time, I felt so much peace in what made no sense to my logical brain. I even questioned if it was normal that I moved around so much. I had been on a wild adventure the last few years and it wasn't about to slow down. I had given God my *yes* and I intended to keep saying *yes*. I had the same familiar peace about going to California that I had when I thought about moving to Oklahoma and going to Guatemala. Sure enough, the Lord was calling me out to ministry school in Redding, California.

CHAPTER 3: PROCESS

What is your heart's deepest cry? Usually on the other side of that answer is an invitation to plunge into the depths of trusting God. When you say *yes* to Jesus, you jump on the tube and ride down the river. You don't know what rapids may be ahead or where it will take you but you know it's going to be a fun adventure.

It takes faith to leave behind what's comfortable and adventure into the unknown. Faith is like a muscle and you have to work it out in order for it to become stronger. Muscles tear down during a workout and rebuild themselves stronger than before using the nutrients that you feed your body. Your faith is like a muscle, your circumstances and the waiting is the workout, and what you believe and speak are the nutrients that make your faith grow stronger.

Some days I'm able to fully let go and trust God and other days I have to back up and figure out where did I lose my peace before I can resolve it and move on. Trust is grown in the beautiful surrender of fully letting go of all control and allowing God to do what He intends to do in you. There is no depth, no height, no end to how deep we can go in trusting God and increasing our faith. There are always new measures of faith and experiences that require the stretching and strengthening of our faith. We may find ourselves in a new situation or circumstance that grows a deeper level of faith than we had before.

It always sounds exhilarating to trust God because we were made to trust and believe Him for the impossible. It is when we are put in a situation that looks impossible; the truth of what we really believe comes to surface. You hear a great sermon, you get on fire, and you say, "Yes Jesus, take me wherever, invade every part of my life, your will be done, have your way!" Then trials come. Money stops coming in like you thought it would. Relationships go sour. Changes come and projects end. How do you respond in these moments? You can either get frustrated and angry with God because what's going on around you doesn't look the way you thought it would or you can trust that He is in control and is calling you to a deeper level of trust.

Sometimes you go through trials because it tests your foundation. In order to go where God wants you to go, you have to pass these tests so that you can handle what He wants to pour out and bestow on you. What are some trials you are going through right now? How are you responding to them?

I love to look back at how I would have handled certain situations a couple of years ago versus how I handle a situation today. I remember things that would completely unravel my world and leave me lost, confused, and distraught. It would take me months sometimes to climb out of that kind of a hole. Surveying how far you have come is a really helpful tool for measuring your growth. Celebrate with me today and say out loud, "I am growing! I am becoming resilient!"

RESPONSIBILITY VS. TRUST

For many of us responsibility is something that has been driven into our heads from a young age. Maybe you grew up with parents that worked constantly and you didn't get to see them much. Or you may have grown up with sayings like: "If you don't work and get educated you won't get anywhere in life," or "You can't live on free handouts," or "Who will put the bread on the table if no one is bringing home the bacon?" Although there is truth in the fact that God honors hard work and He honors due diligence, there is also another side to the coin: idolizing work. When you start putting your work before family and God that is when it becomes a problem.

What do you do if God tells you to quit your job? What do you do when you are unemployed and looking for jobs and can't get hired and the bills start to pile up? Will you trust that He sees something so much bigger than you do?

Ultimately, all provision comes from the Lord. He owns all money and He lacks nothing. Sometimes His provision looks like a job, or a check in the mail, or a new business idea, or someone supporting your ministry and dreams. Sometimes God closes the door on one opportunity because He has something better in store. Other times, He will take you through a season of learning your identity doesn't come from what you do.

One day I was getting a financial Sozo and the Lord taught me something that I will never forget. Sozo is a Greek word, which means healed, saved, and delivered (source #4). Having a Sozo means that you are ministered to through another person's ability to counsel you by the Holy Spirit's leading in seeking deliverance and healing. Usually you are asked a series of questions that help you get to the root issue. I kept going through a cycle of fear regarding my finances and I wanted to get past that point.

As I was going through my financial Sozo God brought up the parable of the prodigal son and the older brother. He said,

"You have a battle going on inside you of the older and younger brother. The older brother's name is 'responsibility' and it's the voice that pushes you, says that I won't come through, that you have to work more and harder, that you need to take matters into your own hands, that I cannot be trusted. The other voice is that of the younger brother that is trusting and says, 'Trust God, He will come through, even if this doesn't make sense'." It finally made sense to me why I was feeling tossed from side to side and in turmoil.

There were days that I would completely trust the Lord, even when it made no sense. Then there were days that I wanted to grab the reins and make things happen in my life. Everything that you are going through is in preparation for what is yet to come. The trials and tests are bringing you to higher grounds. While you are learning to trust Him with what He is doing now, He has something even greater coming for you.

Navigating hearing God's voice comes with practice. His voice is peaceful, loving, kind, confident, and sure. His voice is never heavy, condemning or domineering. Some ways that God can speak to us is: audibly, through a "knowing" at the center of your being (some people refer to this as "trusting your gut"), through peace, visions, dreams, numbers, parables, nature, other people, the Bible, music, movies, and riddles. These are just a few examples but we can't put Him in a box because there are so many facets and ways that He communicates. He created everything; therefore He can speak through everything. He is always speaking but are we listening? Ask God how He is speaking to you today?

It is important to discern the Lord's voice from other thoughts we are influenced by. For example, I would often hear a voice saying to be responsible and work harder and work more. At first I thought this was the Lord's voice because it sounded responsible but it always left me feeling heavy, so I knew that was not His voice. I had to realize that what I thought was His voice was not, but it was a familiar voice I grew up with: the voice of responsibility and performance. God was actually inviting me into a season of rest so that I could focus on other dreams and create space to write this book.

Even though it looked scary financially, I remembered my personal history with God and the countless times God asked me to come into the unknown and how He never failed me. I reflected on the decisions that looked so scary, but once I had peace to do them, I can now see how faithful God was through those decisions. Those moments in my history helped me to navigate and get me where I am today.

SABBATICAL SHEMITTAH

As I was praying during my summer after my 2nd year of ministry about the new season the Lord told me to take a sabbatical *Shemittah*. I did some research because I didn't know what that word meant. I love when God sends me on a treasure hunt to seek out the deeper meaning of things. In Jewish culture in the Old Testament every seven years the people went into *Shemittah*, which means to cease from work. *Shmita* in Hebrew means to release. A cease and release season for the Lord. This was the time when the land would rest so it could recover for a greater harvest in the future. Any fruit that was produced during *Shemittah* was considered ownerless and anyone could pick it. This was also a time of a deeper testing of faith with God (source #5). I believe the time of testing refers to trusting God to provide without the normal means of harvesting.

As a naturally driven, hard working person, this wasn't the easiest word for me to respond to. I used to have an incredibly hard time resting and would feel anxious if I had a day with absolutely nothing to do. I always thought it looked lazy to take a sabbatical but yet in the deepest places of my heart, I had been crying out for extended rest. I wanted at least one of my years of ministry school to be completely focused on God without having to juggle work and school. I would say my body showed the first signs of needing rest this last year as I started having major problems with my thyroid. I've had a condition called hypothyroidism for over 10 years. I am still believing for my thyroid to be fully healed.

Last year my thyroid suddenly went into hyperthyroidism and I had a Graves Disease response called Thyroid Eye Disease. My body went into an autoimmune response and started to attack the tissue behind my eyes causing my eyes to bulge and swell. It was very painful because my eyes would swell every night and I would wake up with incredible pain that would last throughout the day. I had been pushing myself to keep up with an unreasonable pace and I hadn't allowed myself to rest.

I began a journey of learning how to let myself rest and recover. I began finding what brought me rest and made me come alive. I watched the things that filled me up and made them a priority. I started to see a slow healing process take place within my body. To this day my eye is still in the process of healing but it has healed and improved so much!

I had to learn how to maintain a mind stayed on peace. There were days I would be in this "rest" from working but my mind would be filled with anxieties on how I was going to pay the bills or what other people thought about me. During this time God uprooted more lies that I believed. I actually had the time and space to take note of the lies and replace them with truth. This is a process I am still learning how to balance between rest and work. It looks different in different seasons. That is why having relationship with God is so important. Be in communication with Him about your season.

When I enter into His rest and His promise to provide, my body is at peace, my mind is not confused, and I am able to fall back into His open arms. When I am opposing His rest, my body feels tight, I often get back pain from the tension, and I have a hard time making decisions. Rest is a state of mind. You can be incredibly busy but your mind is at rest or you can have nothing to do and your mind is running.

These are some examples of the ways I have been able to indicate if I'm off track. God often speaks to me through my body or a "knowing" in my core. We are connected beings: soul, body, and spirit and they all affect one another. When I feel anxious or not at rest my body indicates this by being tense or having back pain. My mind usually feels cloudy and confused. I'll have a hard time carrying on conversations and will forget what I'm talking about because my mind is preoccupied on something else. I have a hard time making decisions because my mind is not at rest. I'm hoping this will help someone understand what you are feeling in your body and being able to connect with what you're thinking about. We are called to trust in what God is saying even when it doesn't make sense.

THE LAND OF PLENTY RAIN

I was in the prayer house at Bethel Church and I was seeking God on a decision. I was very torn inside because my logic was telling me one thing but my spirit was saying to trust what God. I knew there was peace if I just let go and surrendered to what God wanted to do in my life. I was in turmoil, as my flesh and spirit literally were at odds and colliding. As I walked into the bathroom the Lord dropped Deuteronomy 11 into my head. I picked a spot to sit in the prayer house and opened my Bible and began reading. I was astonished at how directly that chapter spoke right to my season. The whole chapter was exactly what I felt in my spirit God was inviting me into.

"For the land you are about to enter and take over is not like the land of Egypt from which you came, where you planted your seed and made irrigation ditches with your foot as in a vegetable garden. 11 Rather, the land you will soon take over is a land of hills and valleys with plenty of rain—12 a land that the LORD your God cares for. He watches over it through each season of the year" (Deuteronomy 11:10-12 NLT).

I knew what this verse meant for me because in the past I had always dug my "irrigation ditches" but this time I was going into a land that had "plenty of rain" that the Lord cared for. I took that verse as confirmation that I wasn't to get a regular job during my final year of ministry school. I decided to do a more in-depth study on what these verses were actually saying.

In Egypt the land was flat and the people were dependent on the overflow from the Nile to water their crops. So they would dig irrigation ditches to catch the overflow water from the Nile River, which would provide water for their crops. This kind of work was really hard on people's health because they could be waist deep in muddy water. It was very restricting work because they were unable to travel due to constantly tending to the irrigation ditches. Egypt's riches relied on skill and labor, while the Promised Land was a gift from God. The Promised Land they entered was a "land of hills and valleys" and was dependent on the rain from Heaven to water the crops. This signifies a constant dependence on God for the fruitfulness of the land.

The Israelites no longer had to work in the irrigation ditches; they trusted God to bring the former and latter rains. Former and latter rains refer to rain that comes to water the seed and rain that comes at harvest time. Because the Promised Land was watered from Heaven, they were able to travel because they no longer needed to tend to the irrigation ditches.

In Deuteronomy 11:16-17 (NLT) it goes on to say, "But be careful. Don't let your heart be deceived so that you turn away from the Lord and serve and worship other gods. If you do, the Lord's anger will burn against you. He will shut up the sky and hold back the rain, and the ground will fail to produce its harvests. Then you will quickly die in that good land the Lord is giving you." The Israelites had to be obedient to what God had said because obedience to His Word was their source of strength to go in and take over the new land. Their obedience was also the prerequisite for the blessing to be released. God promised He would bring the former and latter rains on condition of their obedience. Bill Johnson, Senior Pastor of Bethel Church, often says, "Physical obedience releases spiritual breakthrough."

The months that followed this word were a lot like a baby learning how to walk. It was awkward to not have a job; it went against every value I was raised on. When people asked me what I did, how was I going to respond? Would I feel empty or less than because I wasn't working? What would I do with all of my time? Had my identity been tied up in what I did?

These are some questions that ran through my mind. As I worked through all of the questions and wondering, I found at my very core that God was truly asking me to not work but to rest.

Some days I did really good with my season and rested in knowing He would provide everything I needed when I needed it. Other times I would grab the reigns and frantically start looking for jobs. During this time I actually applied to several jobs, was given a few interviews, and even offered a couple of jobs. My flesh was screaming, *"Take the job!!! What are you thinking?"* But deep inside the pit of my stomach I knew if I took one of these jobs I would be disobedient to what God was asking of me in that season. I was having a hard time trusting Him and was experiencing a lot of doubt that He would actually come through.

Through the lens of the world this looked like the most idiotic thing to do but to God this looked like the greatest trust building exercise. Despite all the advice that I was getting, I wanted to obey His voice above all the others. I realized I had actually prayed for a season like this. My exact words were: "I want to be so utterly dependent on you God for my every need." He was answering my prayer.

The fear of God requires obedience to what He is saying, which gives us strength and confidence for the blessing He desires to give us.

"Nothing is required of you but obedience to His Word. Be as a young child and step out in confidence, knowing that with your hand in Mine you will always be safe and blessing will attend you," said Frances J. Roberts in his devotional book, *Come Away My Beloved* (source #6). During the sabbatical season where I was not working I revisited the question with the Lord several times during that period to make sure I was still in the same season. As time went on He provided babysitting jobs for me here and there to cover some of my bills. The rest of my expenses were always covered either through a check in the mail, odd job, or from donations from financial supporters. I believe it is wisdom to be fully aware of the season you are in and be in constant communication with the Lord about it. That is why relationship with Him is crucial.

TAKING OVER LAND

Almost exactly a year later I kept seeing the number 1:11 everywhere and kept asking the Lord what it meant. I remembered the past season which I regularly saw 11:11 and how Deuteronomy 11:11 was my verse for that season. I figured there was a reason why I was now seeing 1:11. While visiting my family in Oklahoma I was driving home and heard the Lord say Joshua 1:11.

As soon as I got home I opened my Bible to Joshua 1:11 (NLT), "Go through the camp and tell the people to get their provisions ready. In three days you will cross the Jordan River and take possession of the land the Lord your God is giving you." I had a steady flow of pet sitting, babysitting, and nanny jobs that provided for me to "get my provisions ready." I paid off some small debt I had occurred that came from some decisions I made in fear during ministry school.

I highly suggest going through the book of Joshua because it is a book that can apply to any season of your life. Before Joshua and the armies crossed the Jordan River to the Promised Land the Lord instructed him to be very brave and courageous. Actually, this command appears several times throughout Joshua. Why do you think God kept repeating those words? *Fear not.* God knew Joshua would need those words for the journey he was about to go on. Oftentimes in life in order to get to our Promised Land we have to face some pretty big giants. "Often the guard dogs of doom stand at the doors of destiny," says Kris Vallotton, Senior Associate Leader of Bethel Church. There may be scary circumstances before your destiny but you have supernatural courage and bravery to confront any circumstance or giant in your life.

An interesting fact I learned while studying the journey of the Israelites taking their land in Joshua was that they were tent people. They did not make their homes in the wilderness during the wilderness journey. They put up a tent and moved to the next city when the Lord said to move. Then God would give them the land and their descendants occupied the land. At every city the Israelites had multiple battles and seemingly impossible circumstance to overcome first. They went from Egypt, to the wilderness, to Shittim, to crossing the Jordan River, to Gilgal, to Jericho, to Ai, to Gilgal, and then finally, to their Promised Land.

At each city giants stood there and the situation looked impossible but God gave them revelation and strategies of how to defeat their enemies. Even though the Israelites had made some messes and had not asked God about certain decisions, His promises still prevailed. I don't know about you but that brings comfort to me. It shows me that God is big enough to still bring us into our destinies, even if we make mistakes. It also reassures me that we can't miss our destiny. His Word does not return void.

God brought them through every impossible circumstance with a radical supernatural occurrence. He parted two bodies of water for them supernaturally, the Red Sea and the Jordan

River. Every time they came to a new city that the Lord wanted to give them, they had to listen specifically to how He wanted them to take the land. It was different every time. What worked at the Red Sea didn't work at the Jordan. Everywhere they went they carried the Ark of the Covenant, which represented God's presence. God is relational and He never wants us to brave our Promised Land alone. He promises to never leave or forsake you. His presence is always with you. *We need to be strong, brave, and courageous and not give into fear or back down when we are entering our land.*

God had already performed the miracles of manna and daily trust to humble and test the Israelites in building their character. The Israelites needed this season for where they were going. God provided the miracles so that the Israelites could take those memorial stones and remember what He had done in the past the next time they faced an obstacle that looked impossible. He wants to build us up so that we are fully trusting in Him and not other idols. We need these seasons in order to go in and take our Promised Land.

God then warns the Israelites not to forget who it was that brought them into the Promised Land. "But that is the time to be careful (once you reach your Promised Land)! Beware that in your plenty you do not forget the Lord your God and disobey his commands" (Deuteronomy 8:11 NLT parenthesis added).

How I know this pains His heart. He longs to give us the Promised Land but He doesn't want us to forget who brought us into the Promised Land and who provides for us in every season, whether it is of plenty or little. We need Him if not more in the season of plenty than in the season of lack.

In order to enter your Promised Land, it requires taking action steps with great courage. Courage is often defined as: doing the thing you are most afraid of, while feeling the fear.

The old saying "He can't do much with a parked car" is true. It is action that makes our faith count. "In the same way, faith by itself, if it is not accompanied by action, is dead" (James 2:17 NLT).

An example of faith being accompanied by action can be seen in Joshua 3. In this section, the priests had to step into the Jordan River for it to dry up. We have to have action as we move forward in faith. I wonder how differently it would have happened if the priests had waited for God to dry the river before moving forward. They didn't wait; they put their feet in and upon that act of faith the river dried up. Once again the Lord performs a mighty miracle and causes the river to backup and become dry so that the Israelites can cross the river. This is the second time God caused a massive body of water to dry up so the Israelites could cross over it. Think on that for a moment. A roaring river was suddenly dried up once their feet hit the water! That is incredible! Talk about supernatural. Those massive bodies of water represent the impossibilities in our life that God longs to show Himself faithful, and through His miraculous power the impossibilities become possible.

As the Israelites witnessed supernatural acts of God He instructs them to set up memorial stones as reminders for the future generations. God works in generations and has a plan for eternity. What He longs for is a person who treasures and recalls the testimonies of His faithfulness in their lives so that they can pass it down to their children and children's children. God wants us to progress—His heart is not for us to go backwards but that we continue to be propelled forward and keep building upon what the previous generation left us. In our own lives we also need memorial stones that remind us just how faithful God is and how many times in the past that He has come through.

THE IMPORTANCE OF REST

Rest has become something that I hold such a high value for, that I get very protective over my rest time. This is because I used to not value rest and only valued production and overworking myself until I would crash. One of the many things I learned in ministry school is that we are called to run a long race; think marathon, not a sprint.

So if you don't give yourself time to rest and push through ministry and disregard sleep, recharge time, fun, eating well, and exercise you end up paying for it down the road. No one wants to burn out early or not make it in the long run, so implementing a lifestyle of rest is so important. Now I actually schedule rest into my week, as well as fun and adventure time. Many depression and anxiety issues would be relieved over learning a lifestyle of rest, fun, and adventure.

The way I became self aware of what recharged me was by making a list of things that made me feel recharged, full of life, and well rested. Now I have a list in my phone that I can look at to get some ideas of what I can do to recharge. Learning to rest was not something that happened over night. Especially with me being a "Type A" personality. Learning to rest and not always "do, do, do" had to be unlearned because it was so deeply wired within me to always produce.

Resting is a state of mind. How do we enter into the rest of the Lord? We can enter into physical rest as well as mental rest. Physical rest is something that can often be overlooked until we are past the point of exhaustion. Mental rest means your mind is at peace and clear. Not full of anxious thoughts or confusion. Have you ever noticed that you feel completely at peace and then something happens and you go into striving mode or feeling like you're carrying the weight of the issue?

When that happens, you've just left rest and went into strive mode. Your body needs physical rest but you also have to be at rest mentally. Start paying attention to when these patterns happen in your life. The first step of change is being aware.

I was sick for a week with the flu. I had no energy to do anything, I couldn't even watch a movie I was that sick. I let my body rest and sleep. I turned on worship music and laid in bed for hours as I listened to the music. The following days I was still not feeling well enough to put forth much energy and something happened in me during those days. I let go of all the worries and striving because I didn't have the energy to keep up with all the demands on my life. I didn't have the energy to petition and declare anything. I was silent.

Then a few days later I completely lost my voice and was left in a state of silence. The most interesting thing happened though; I could hear God's voice perfectly clear. My mind was calm, my body was still, and my ears were listening for Him because I wasn't so busy petitioning and declaring for things. I thought to myself, *how often am I talking too much and not giving God the space or room to speak to me?*

I have been on missions trips where rest was non-existent and the attitude of "We are only here for two weeks, we can sleep when we get home" was implemented. I agree with going hard on a mission trip but I don't agree with pushing yourself to the limit where you get sick or come back from a mission trip completely depleted. There is a balance between pushing yourself and having long days but also being able to recuperate and sleep. There are times when you will feel tired and you will need to push through and then there are times when you need to pull back and rest. The best way to balance this is by knowing your body and asking Holy Spirit. You know your body better than anyone. When you continue to push through and don't give your body time to rest or sleep enough that is when you end up with exhaustion or sickness. We are physical human beings and everything is connected together.

Being someone who is wired to "war," rest was something that got put on the back shelf because it wasn't important to me. If we are always warring, we are not giving ourselves time to rest and recover. There is a beautiful balance between going to war and knowing when to lie down and rest like Psalm 23 talks about. My usual is to be a warrior and push through hard circumstances and never give up. It has taken me years to learn that I don't have to always be in fight mode but that I can lie down because the battle has already been won.

If you were stripped of all of your callings, destiny, and promises, if you ceased from every work, what would you be left with? If that question is scary for you, as it was for me, you might want to take some time and figure out why. What is at your core when you are not producing something?

Alone time is really important so you can listen to God, process, and get direction from Him alone. If you can't be alone for a period of time that is another deeper issue. It could be that you don't like yourself, you don't enjoy your own company, or you don't like the thoughts that are produced during times alone. When you are alone with nothing to do that is when the overflow of the heart really speaks.

What thoughts are you entertaining? Do you enjoy being with yourself or do you have to stay busy and occupied so you don't have to think about everything that comes up?

Avoidance is not the way to grow. You have to confront and address these issues in order to grow fully into the person you are called to be. If you enjoy yourself and can be alone, you have discovered the beauty that your self-talk is really healthy and positive because you can be alone without the fear of what might come up.

SEASONS AND KNOWING THE ONE YOU'RE IN

In every season of life we must know what God is saying. This gives us confidence to move in the direction God is taking us. Even when God speaks against our logical, rational mindsets we must respond and obey His voice. He will never lead us astray nor will He abandon us. I love to remember this promise when I'm doing something that God is leading me to do but the people around me don't agree with it, or think I am crazy. "No one who trusts in you will ever be put to shame" (Psalm 25:3 The Amplified Bible). "And they who know Your name [who have experience and acquaintance with Your mercy] will lean on and confidently put their trust in You, for You, Lord have not forsaken those who seek (inquire of and for) You [on the authority of God's Word and the right of their necessity]" (Psalm 9:10 The Amplified Bible).

What may have worked for you before may not be what works for you now. One day can mark a new season; seasons can change that fast. God will let you know what season you are in if you ask Him. There is a time and place for everything. There are seasons where He is teaching you the value of excellence and hard work. There are seasons where He is teaching you to rest. He may ask you to fast or not do anything and let Him bring it to you. You can tire yourself out by not knowing what season you are in. What is the word God has spoken to you about your season?

WILDERNESSES AND WHAT TO DO WHEN YOU'RE IN ONE

Post graduation from ministry school I went through a

really interesting transition. It was a bit uncomfortable as I had just went through three years of being told how great I was, received all of these prophetic words and promises, and then all of a sudden—a halt. I was babysitting and still in Redding with no real purpose. It was so strange to have finished a 3-year ministry school, have a college degree, a successful career—and to what? To be babysitting? But yet, that is what I had grace to do. I was in the crux of transition. I had finished one season but had not yet entered the next. I wrote this in my journal:

"My time at BSSM was like a hand crafted wine that was perfected by time, squeezing, pressing, bottling, and now being set aside to age. I have to remember that He saves the best for last. Good wine takes time to age. While people may take the other bottles to enjoy now, they leave the special wine for special occasions. At the right time they open the well-aged wine. Even if I feel like I've been set on the shelf, I'm still aging and becoming even better tasting with time. So be it."

Every person who did something great in the Bible went through obscurity and multiple wilderness seasons. God gave these heroes great callings and dreams that they would one day fulfill, but first He took them through a refining process. This process can be so painful and often feel like you've been forgotten or left behind as you watch those around you walk into their destiny. You begin to ask yourself, "What about me?" or "What did I do wrong?" In these seasons, you have to remember this is part of the process of becoming great. Anything that would hinder you or hold you back begins to get pressed and squeezed out of you during seasons like this.

As Lisa Bevere, speaker and author, said in one of her recent podcasts, "It's not one wilderness you go through in life, it's multiple wildernesses. There are different preparations.

You do not sit down and cry and camp out and build a home in your wilderness. You are passing through it on the way to your Promised Land" (source #7). Like the Israelites who complained, their story was used to warn us and be an example so that we would not fall into the same condition of complaining but realize that God is moving us through our wilderness into our Promised Land. There is a test that comes with seasons of lack and barrenness as well as one that comes with prosperity. May you allow God to do what He needs to do and take no shortcuts so that you can be everything He wants you to be—perfected by trials, times, and wilderness seasons.

God speaks a lot to me through warrior movies. Recently, I re-watched Snow White and the Huntsman and saw King Arthur for the first time. (King Arthur was a bit dark for me so I would not suggest watching it if you are highly sensitive.) Both Snow White and King Arthur were of noble birth and evil queens and kings had stripped their identity away from them when they were younger. This is similar to how the enemy tends to target people's childhoods and strip them from their identity at a young age—he fears who they will become. They both were given the chance to take back their kingdom and royal birthright but first they had to go through their own battles and wildernesses in order to have the authority to take back their Kingdom.

Snow White had to go through the dark forest and fought many battles on the way to reach her destiny moment. Most people died in the dark forest because it fed off people's weaknesses and usually consumed them but Snow White makes it through the forest. Even though she made it through the dark forest, she still had other battles ahead that she had to conquer on the way to regaining her Kingdom and healing the land. She even faced death. It was after making it through every battle on her journey to her Promised Land that she had one final battle in which she had to take back her Kingdom from the evil queen. (This story reminds me a lot of the journey the Israelites went on in the book of Joshua. They encountered several battles on the way to their Promised Land.) After she arises from death she adorns an army together to help her fight the evil queen and then she makes this beautiful bold speech to rally her people:

"Iron will melt, but it will writhe inside of itself! All these years, all I've known is darkness. But I have never seen a brighter light than when my eyes just opened. And I know that light burns in all of you! Those embers must turn to flame. Iron into sword! I will become your weapon! Forged with a fierce fire that I know is in your hearts! For I have seen what she sees, I know what she knows. I can kill her. And I'd rather die today than live another day of this death! And who will ride with me? Who will be my brother?" (source #8)

Think about it, you have the light of Jesus that burns within you. The fire of God is inside of you, which turns iron into a sword. It is your weapon that becomes forged with the fire that is inside of your heart. Your sword is your weapon to defeat the enemy.

In the second movie I mentioned above, King Arthur had to go through the Darklands in order to be prepared to take over the throne of the evil King. Most people also died in the Darklands but King Arthur makes it through even though he is severely injured and yet gains authority to take over the evil King. Do you notice a theme here? You must go through the hard times of testing and have some grit to persevere in order to gain authority for where you're going. I'm pretty sure there's a verse like that. James 1:3-4 (NLT) says, "For you know that when your faith is tested, your endurance has a chance to grow. So let it grow, for when your endurance is fully developed, you will be perfect and complete, needing nothing."

Even Jesus went through a wilderness and then came out with authority. Every person who goes through the wilderness arises with authority. Jesus went through the wilderness of testing and used the Word of God as His sword to combat the lies of His enemy. Once Jesus finished His time in the wilderness He had gained a new level of authority. "Then Jesus returned to Galilee, filled with the Holy Spirit's power" (Luke 4:14 NLT). From this point on we see Jesus step into His ministry. Look at the characters of the Bible like Paul, Joseph, David, and Jonah. They were sent into slavery, prison, deserts, obscurity and a whale's belly before they walked in their Promised Land.

Your wilderness may look different depending on what God is preparing you for. But oftentimes your toughest season is what produces your life message. In one of John and Lisa Bevere's recent podcasts, they define wilderness as: "Any part of your life that feels far from the promises of God. You're wondering 'God, where are you?' It feels like you can not see your way out and you are furthest from your promises" (source #7).

Oftentimes as you get ready to enter your Promised Land fear and lies will attempt to take you out. I wrote this excerpt in my journal:

Fear will try to immobilize you or get you to act out in a state of self-protection before its time. Its loud voice will scream at you and constantly nag you to "Go do something! Make it happen! Quit waiting! You're being lazy! You'll be in lack! God won't come through!" But you assert your authority and tell the devil you do not get to speak to me. Only God tells me who I am and only God directs me on what to do.

Ishmaels are made in fear and control based choices. Isaacs are made supernaturally by trusting the Lord to bring about the promise.

One day the Lord spoke to me and said, "Distraction brings destruction." I asked, "What does that mean?" He answered, "The enemy knows he can no longer get you to sin in areas that used to be a struggle for you but now he will try to distract you from what I have in store for you. He will present himself like an angel of light in the forms of good and better opportunities. All in hopes that you miss the best opportunity that I have in store for you." If he can get you to settle into a certain job so that you don't reach your full potential or settle for marrying a guy who is not God's best for you, then he can take you out. He tries to destroy through distraction.

It is most important to be highly vigilant and discerning when opportunities arise. Especially when you are in a transition season. Opportunities will arise that seem great but you must wait for the best opportunity to come—the one that you know is the best from God. The one your spirit confirms with by having peace and a *yes, this is what I have been waiting for.*

Sylvia Gunter and Arthur Burk sum this up beautifully in their book *Blessing Your Spirit* (source #9).

"Your Father will bless you, (insert your name)_____ with the right closed doors, because your enemy will try to get you to do things that God has not designed you to do—good things, legitimate things, profitable things, honorable things, but your Father has not designed you to do them. I bless you with not wasting time or effort in doing things that God has not called you to do, but being able to invest fully where God is positioning you and being fully present to today's grace and today's

assignment. Your Father will bless you with open doors to walk forward in His time, in His calling, for you to experience the joy of fulfillment of being everything He has called you to be at the right time and in the right place."

"Stand at attention while I prepare you for your work. I'm making you as impregnable a castle, immovable as a steel post, solid as a concrete block wall" (Jeremiah 1:18 The Message Translation). Through keeping your eyes fixed on Jesus you will be prepared to face anything that comes your way. Be attentive while God prepares you for where you're going. Fix your eyes on Jesus and distractions will fall off.

LOGOS AND RHEMA WORD

We must know what God has said, is currently saying, and what His Word says. Faith requires knowing the logos Word of God, which are His promises in the Bible and what the Word says. The rhema word is the freshly spoken word of God or the prophetic word of God. To get a better understanding of what rhema and logos words are I'm going to explain them below.

The Greek meaning of rhema is "utterance." Rhema words can be prophetic words that you get from others, when God is speaking directly to your spirit, or when God speaks audibly to you. In Matthew 4:4 (NLT, emphasis added) Jesus says, "Man shall not live by bread alone, but by every word [rhema] that proceeds out of the mouth of God." In John 6:63 (NLT, emphasis added) Jesus again is referring to the rhema word of God in the following passage: "The words [rhema] that I speak to you are spirit, and they are life." The rhema word over Jesus' life was the cross. He knew where He was going and every move He made was based on knowing His destiny. He did nothing apart from the Father. He communed with Him and listened for His voice, guidance, and instructions. Jesus had a prophetic vision over His life and nothing could stop Him from fulfilling that word.

We need to know what God is saying in order to know where we are going. When people falter, compromise, or become despondent and depressed it is because they have lost vision for their life. Proverbs 29:18 sum this up beautifully, I love how it is written in the English Standard Version: "Where there is no prophetic vision the people cast off restraint, but blessed is he who keeps the law." When God speaks a rhema word to us, it creates life. You know your purpose, destiny, and why you are on this earth. Once you know God's vision for your life, funnel every decision through that lens. Our *yes* becomes greater than our *no* as we have a better idea of what we are being called to. We are able to filter the opportunities, decisions, and choices that are presented to use through these words.

"The meaning of *logos* in Greek is translated as "word," "speech," "principle," or "thought." In Greek philosophy, logos is referred to as a universal, divine reason or the mind of God" (source #10). The Trinity is also the logos word of God because it existed before time and before the universe was created. "In the beginning was the Word, and the Word was with God, and the Word was God. He was in the beginning with God. All things were made through Him, and without Him was not any thing made that was made. In Him was life, and the life was the light of men" (John 1:1-4 ESV).

Think about this: before you were ever born, you were a thought in God's mind. He knew that you would be born into the world on a certain date at a certain time with a seed planted inside your soul for what you were created to accomplish on this earth. He had a plan long before we were living human beings. Every single person has a purpose and a destiny. Calling out people's destiny is so important, so they know who they are and who God created them to be. He loved and chose you first (Ephesians 1:4) but you get to decide if you'll choose him back. Because He is a God of love, He allows us to ultimately accept to co-labor with Him or to reject Him.

One of our core values from Bethel School of Supernatural Ministry is: God still speaks today. Because we have the Holy Spirit inside of us, we have access to the voice of God. The Creator of the Universe lives inside of me. Therefore, I have access to all wisdom and all knowledge. My pastor Bill Johnson often says, "There is no problem or situation He doesn't have an answer for".

God longs for us to ask Him what He is doing and to give us direction and purpose in our life. When we have the word of the Lord whether it is a logos word or a rhema word, we have a weapon of warfare. The Word of God is known as the sword; therefore by declaring, believing, and acting on the Word of God we are able to stand confident no matter what circumstance comes our way. This is our battle weapon against anything that opposes the Word of God. Author, speaker, and pastor Steve Backland, of Igniting Hope says, "Just like Abraham we are to speak God's promises over our lives."

Proverbs 18:21 (NLT), "Life and death are in the power of the tongue." What are you saying about your situation? Are you saying this is impossible, God won't come through, this is too hard, this sickness, disease, or poverty is God's will for my life? Or are you saying the truth that God will always come through and never fail me, I can do all things through Christ, I am called to be prosperous, wealthy, and not in lack. By Jesus' stripes all sickness, disease, poverty, and lack are already paid for. He said it is already finished. We need to get into agreement with what He says and stand confidently on the Word of God.

Bill Johnson often says, "The prophetic word of God has to go through testing". When you look at the promises that were spoken over Sarah and Abraham, Joseph, David, and others we see that they were all given a promise from God but they went through the testing of their character before it was time for the prophetic word to come to pass. "Until the time came to fulfill his dreams, the Lord tested Joseph's character" (Psalm 105:19 New American Standard Bible). The testing of our faith produces endurance, character, and strengthens our confidant hope of salvation. We need this type of testing in order to be complete and lacking nothing.

DEEPER STILL

I thought that I trusted God and had great faith but He took me even deeper. I had no job, no money, and knew no one in California. The only thing I knew was that I was to attend ministry school at Bethel. I had sold most of my belongings and packed up two suitcases of stuff and shipped a box or two to California and went back to Guatemala for the summer before flying to Redding, California. I got to spend three months in the country I loved before I headed out to ministry school.

When I arrived during a blazing hot Redding summer it was super uncomfortable at first. I had no car and I got a part-time job at the local school where I was making what I made in high school. Talk about a blow to your pride! There were times that I was furious with God because I was in the toughest financial situation of my life. Plus, I didn't know why I wasn't on the mission field, which is where I wanted to be. I had followed

God and trusted Him and kept feeling that I was hitting my head against a concrete wall. Nothing I was doing was working and the wall in my life would not budge. I was confused because I knew I was supposed to be in ministry school but financially it looked like a really bad idea to stay. It's good to be real with God. Have a conversation with Him and let out all your emotions. He can handle it!

A perspective shift occurred about half-way through the year when I realized that God had already given me authority over my situation and instead of praying orphan prayers where I was begging God to do something for me, I started declaring what His Word says. I saw the power of declarations, as I declared the following verses over my life.

- Matthew 6:26 (NLT): "Look at the birds. They don't plant or harvest or store food in barns, for your heavenly Father feeds them. And aren't you far more valuable to him than they are?"

- Matthew 6:33 (NLT): "Seek the Kingdom of God above all else, and live righteously, and he will give you everything you need."

- Philippians 4:19 (NLT): "And this same God who takes care of me will supply all your needs from his glorious riches, which have been given to us in Christ Jesus."

Looking in my bare cupboard I had one sweet potato and a banana left to eat. I had no money and no idea how I would eat tomorrow. I was learning a whole new meaning of "daily manna". God promised me He would always provide, but it was not always in the time frame I liked. As author Max Lucado says, "God meets daily needs daily. Not weekly or annually. He will give you what you need when it is needed."

The following day I would always have food. I would have random checks come in the mail, people would hand me money, I would get gift cards to restaurants and grocery stores, and I even received backdated insurance money. It wasn't easy to learn this but I began to learn a new side of God's character and provision. ***The one, who feeds the birds of the field, feeds me.***

One day as I was on my prayer walk I noticed birds in the field eating and I was reminded of Matthew 6:26 where God said that He feeds the birds of the field, and that we are much more precious to Him than birds. I said, "Ok God, if you are feeding these birds then surely you are going to feed me." And He always did feed me. He has never failed me, nor will He ever fail you. Now every time I see a bird eating, it's a symbol to me of God's provision.

Learning a new side of God's character can feel foreign and uncomfortable at first. It is exploring the unknown with the deep belief that God is who He says He is. I walked away from my first year of ministry school with a deep understanding of who God was.

Since then I have seen Him come through in so many ways. Time and time again He provided for every single need that I had. I never went without. It may have come down to the last minute but He always did what He said He would do. Some days I would have 10 cents to my name but then He would provide. He would ask me, "Christina, do you have enough for today? Do you have enough gas, food, shampoo, etc?" "Yes," I would say. He would always reply, "Ok then you are good to go. We will talk about tomorrow, tomorrow."

He provided for all of my tuition for all three years of ministry school. Every ministry trip and mission trip I went on during that time was paid for. I even got to go back to

Guatemala for a few months between my first and second year. He provided a car to rent and all my bills were paid every month. Sometimes it was really tough because I was staring lack in the face on a regular basis. There were times when I didn't know how I would eat or make ends meet.

I don't believe that we are meant to live in "just getting by" mode forever or on daily manna forever. I do believe God's ultimate goal is for us to live in abundance and produce wealth. But I do know that God is such a good Father, He knows how to shape and mold His kids so that they become the most successful and well set up people. I wouldn't be surprised if you go through a "daily manna" season at some point in your life. Especially if you are a "type-A" person, overly responsible, or feel the weight of providing rests on your own shoulders. God wants you to live in abundance but also with a light burden not a heavy one.

I am so thankful for that minimal resource season in my life. It taught me to trust God in a way that never would have happened had I not gone through that season. I can now stay in peace regardless of my financial situation. I can come to the due date of a bill and remain in peace knowing that I will be able to pay it.

When I started my first year of ministry school God told me to write down my testimonies so that when I got into a crunch I could go back and re-read what He had done. I still record testimonies to this day and reflect on what He has done. Testimony literally means, "Do it again" in Hebrew. Revelation 19:10 (New King James Version) reads, "The testimony of Jesus is the spirit of prophecy." Whenever you hear a testimony you can say, "God, do that again for me." Whenever you see something God has done for someone else you can know He will do the same thing for you. He is the God of testimony.

"And they have defeated him by the blood of the Lamb and by the word of their testimony" (Revelation 12:11 NLT).

My favorite testimony was from a simple thought that crossed my mind. I was sitting in class thinking about how I would love to shop at Trader Joe's but maybe in this season I would just have to shop at Walmart. I love organic food and eating really healthy but it was also beyond my budget. Then I tuned back into the speaker and kept on going with my day. Shortly after class was over a woman walked up to me and gave me a card. When I opened it, to my surprise, there was $100 gift card to Trader Joe's. God had heard my thoughts! I was brought to tears. God showed me how much He cares that He knows the fleeting thoughts we have.

CHAPTER 4: TRANSFORMING YOUR MIND

According to Romans 8:7 the mind that is not renewed is at war with God. I think one of the biggest challenges we humans face is to get away from rational, make sense, logical thinking when we are following God. Now, I do not mean to not use your brain at all. Don't throw the baby out with the bath water. God gave us beautiful, intelligent, creative, smart, sound-minded brains to use for His good. What I am suggesting is that we don't put God in a box. He is the God of supernatural. He owns cattle on a thousand hills, He raised Jesus from the dead, He parted seas, and He turned water into wine. None of these occurrences seem logical, so we need to remember to allow our spirit to rise above our logical mindsets.

I was such a planner and organized to the point that if something messed up my schedule I would go into a bit of frenzy. Being like that doesn't work too well when you say *yes* to Jesus. Saying *yes* to Him means that He can disrupt your schedule for what He wants to accomplish. The best thing we can do is surrender and allow God to move in our lives in whatever way He wants.

FUZZY FEELINGS

I am going to give you a lesson in Psychology 101. Feelings and actions never precede thoughts. First you start off with a thought, which produces a feeling or emotion, which causes an action. Have you ever noticed when you begin to get anxious it's because of what you are thinking about? Anxiety is future oriented thinking; depression is past oriented thinking. A thought always produces a feeling, which always produces an action. It never goes in any other order. When I found this out it was like I had found a piece of gold. It changed my life. I always thought that I had no control over my anxiety or panic attacks. I found my key to freedom when I realized I could trace my thoughts back to when I first lost my peace and recognize the thought that caused the anxiety. Lies from the enemy will always produce anxiety. The truth will always bring peace.

Once I started realizing when my thoughts got off track I started using several strategies. I would spend time thanking God for what He had already done and I would thank Him for the things I needed as if I already had them. Because we are citizens of Heaven, we already have all that we need in God. I would use declarations and would say them out loud until I came into a place of peace. I would find scripture that applied to my situation and I would declare it out loud.

My all time favorite scripture that helped me defeat anxiety and fear is: 2 Timothy 1:7, "I have not been given a spirit of fear but of power, love, and sound mind." I would repeat this scripture 50 times a day until I believed it. Anything contrary to a sound-mind is not of God; therefore I cannot entertain those kinds of thoughts.

THOUGHT LIFE

Author and speaker Joyce Meyer always says, "Think about what you're thinking about." What a simple yet profound concept. On average we think 50,000 to 70,000 thoughts a day! That's a whole lot of chatter that goes on in our brains throughout the day. Often many of these thoughts are subconscious and routine.

Athena Staik, PhD talks about how soft-wired thoughts are learned through routine and are in our subconscious, while hard-wired thoughts are the ones that were put instinctively in the body. Athena Staik, PhD says, "Information that is soft-wired has been *learned*, and thus can be unlearned or changed. Your thoughts and beliefs fall in this category; you have *learned* them, either consciously or subconsciously, from the time you were first exposed to language. In contrast, information that is hard-wired consists of *unalterable* laws that govern the operation and life of your body, such as inborn drives to survive (physical *and* psychological *self*) and thrive (self in meaningful connection)" (source #11).

Thought processes are like a map in your brain, and once you've learned to think a certain way, certain situations will trigger a thought pattern and will follow the same route as before. This is where people get stuck in bad thinking cycles. If every time you encounter a financial situation and you automatically think: *I am poor, I have no money, I will never make it*, then you have trained your brain to react with a "poverty mentality" when those situations arise. However, you can rewire your brain by thinking: *My bank account is abundant, I am prosperous, I am wealthy and I always have more than enough.*

Rewiring your thought process takes time but as you begin to replace poor thinking with powerful thoughts you will pave new roads in your thought process and it will begin to become your new norm. You have to train your brain how to think. Training is something that takes place over time and it takes consistency, time, and patience to see the desired result.

I have noticed this same mentality when it comes to weightlifting. I love CrossFit and have found that it challenges my mind and body to do the seemingly impossible. If I walk up to a bar loaded with weight and think: *I don't think I am going to get this*, I end up missing the weight. If I walk up to the bar and think: *I am strong, I am going to get this weight, and I can do this*, I almost always hit the weight. That is how I have reached personal records over the last few years. It is incredible what our bodies will do when we put our minds to it. I have felt like I couldn't go one more step while working out, or finish one more rep, but then I changed my mindset, and before I know it, I have completed the workout.

Last weekend I competed in an "in house" CrossFit competition. The first workout was my worst because of the daunting 95-pound atlas stone we had to pick up and set on our shoulders. I tried to get the atlas ball up several times only to keep dropping it on the ground. The weight wasn't the problem because I knew I was strong enough to get the stone up, it was that I couldn't figure out how to lift the ball onto my shoulders. Then I looked around me to see that all the women had the ball up on the shoulders.

I started to think: *I can't get this ball up. I already felt sick today and am not 100%. I should've just stayed home. Oh no! Now look! All the women around me have the ball up except for me. I'm letting my partner down. Wow, I'm weak.* With having that kind of a tape player going in my head you can imagine how the workout went. My partner had to hold the ball while I did the rest of the work because I couldn't hold it. I could barely breathe and then the lovely "3, 2, 1...time!" was shouted and we were finished. I finished the workout wanting to cry and quit. My body was reacting to the thoughts that were going through my mind.

I went into the bathroom to re-group and God said to me, "Christina, you are just getting over being sick. Be kind to yourself. Focus on your breathing and see what happens. Focus on that round. That moment." I went back out for the last three workouts and ended up doing way better than I thought. I was focusing on my thoughts, on breathing calmly, and that I was strong. Everything changed from that first workout. I left that day thinking: *what am I actually capable of if I put my mind to it? I could be unstoppable.*

The thoughts we entertain in our brain are what separate us from the ones who can and the ones who can't. This is why the enemy attacks the mind with thoughts that produce fear and anxiety. God has given us victory. He has given us the power to control our own thoughts. We just have to believe it. **This is one area of life you do have control over: what you allow in your brain.**

We have our own thoughts, God's thoughts, and the devil's thoughts. It is easy to recognize what thoughts come from the devil because they always lead to negative emotions. Once we bring light to the darkness, it has to flee. God's thoughts will always bring peace, reassurance, love, compassion, security, and more. I believe that knowing God's thoughts towards us are always good thoughts because He is entirely good. Our thoughts are more like our personality or your normal everyday thoughts *(I want to go eat at that new pizza place, I love the color blue, I don't like cheese, etc.)* The key here isn't to get too introspective and worry about which thoughts come from whom, it's being aware that not every thought you have is your own. We are called to bring every thought captive. "We destroy arguments and every lofty opinion raised against the knowledge of God; and take every thought captive to obey

Christ" (2 Corinthians 10:5 ESV).

At first I thought the battle to change my thinking would never transform. I would make my declarations every day despite how I felt. I would carry around my medication just in case the panic and anxiety got too intense that I couldn't calm down on my own. I had scripture plastered all over my room, on the mirror in my bathroom, in my car, and on note cards that I would pull out and re-read when I started feeling anxious. I even wrote scripture on my notebooks and planner so that I could have it in front of me during class or at work. I remember thinking I would never get through this or have victory over it. Thank God for Joyce Meyer because after listening to her I had faith that my situation would actually change because hers did.

Today I am living off of the harvest that I planted years ago. I let the Word transform me as I dug up the roots of poor thinking and replaced them with the deep rich soil of scripture. All of that hard work tearing up the soil, digging through it, planting seeds, watering the seeds and pulling up the weeds had finally paid off. My situation did change. I did get victory in my thought life. God had transformed my mind. Now I don't need to have verses plastered everywhere because they are plastered in my heart and mind. They are embedded in my thoughts.

POVERTY MENTALITY

As God continued to reveal mindsets that needed transforming another area came up during this journey when I was experiencing financial lack. I had "poverty mentality," which means I had really poor beliefs and thoughts about finances. *3 Signs of Poverty Mentality* defines "poverty mentality" as "The mindset that believes one is inferior in quality, inadequate in capability, a magnet for failure, and lacking in resources" (source #12). I would nervously beg God to provide for me and was so scared I wouldn't have enough to pay my bills, get groceries, or even have gas to put in the car.

Instead of begging God to break through my situation, I had to remember His promises to provide. I began to declare the opposite of my lack and declare that I had abundance. I thanked God for what I needed as if I already had it. Now, I know some of you are thinking, "name it and claim it does not work." This is not naming and claiming; this is declaring the truth over your circumstances. God's Word does not say we should be in lack but that we have everything we need and He wants to bless us with abundance. I do believe God holds back blessings at times because the magnitude of the blessing would crush us if we weren't ready.

What I am aiming at here is there comes a point when we have to stop praying "orphan prayers" in which we beg our Father to do something for us and start thanking Him and declaring what He has already done for us. We have an inheritance in the Father as Ephesians 1:11 states: "When you believed, you were marked in him with a seal, the promised Holy Spirit, who is a deposit guaranteeing our inheritance until the redemption of those who are God's possession—to the praise of his glory."

Sometimes we go around and around the same mountain because we don't realize the authority we've already been given. When I first started walking with the Lord, I did pray those prayers. "If it's your will, God would you please, etc" and I did see Him answer those prayers but there comes a time as your relationship deepens where the Father asks you to come into alignment with what His Word says. There is a maturity that happens when we come to know God truly as our Heavenly Father. Paul talked about maturity in 1 Corinthians 3:2, saying some people were not spiritually mature, so he gave them milk instead of solid food because they were not ready for it.

WILL THIS EVER CHANGE?

"You may just have to be on medication the rest of your life Christina. Anxiety and depression may just be part of the rest of your life." This was advice that people had told me before when I was going through the rut of anxiety and panic attacks. Yet, it was something much deeper than medication could cover. I do believe there is a time and place to use medication to help imbalances, especially if you are unable to cope with life. There is no shame in using medication and it doesn't mean you aren't strong; everyone's journey is different. But I do want to give you hope that there is freedom from being on anxiety and depression medication. I knew my issue was more of a spiritual one but didn't have the tools to fully break free.

Several months after being on medication I knew God wanted me to get off of it. He said, "It's time to take off the band aid and get to the deeper issue. You are strong enough now to do this work." As I mentioned previously, it was extremely intense work and it felt like it may never change but it did.

When you are allowing your mind to be transformed there are times you will wonder, "Will this ever change?" The enemy would love to tell you it won't or that you are crazy, insane, or something is wrong with you. The most profound thing that was ever said to me during this time was from one a co-worker who was also a pastor. One day we were sitting in a meeting and I was riddled with anxiety. After the meeting he looked over at me and asked if I was okay. I told him I was so anxious and I felt really panicky. He said, "Christina, that anxiety is not you. You have a spirit of peace, love, and sound mind. That is a spirit of fear. It is separate from your spirit. Even though you may feel anxious, that spirit is not yours because you have the Holy Spirit."

The whole time I had been thinking anxiety was part of me, as if something was wrong with me. I never considered that because the Holy Spirit was inside of me, I had a spirit of peace which meant when I felt anxiety it was a spirit of fear trying to attach itself to me. One of the worst things believers can do is water-down the spiritual reality we live in. There are spirits and a real battle that goes on around us. It is Biblical. That piece of freedom He gave me that day was another chain link that had been broken off and I was becoming more and more free.

Believe me, it will change. Give yourself grace because re-training your mind to think differently takes time. Breaking habits take time, as well as breaking thought patterns. "But we do not belong to those who shrink back and are destroyed, but to those who have faith and are saved" (Hebrews 10:39 NIV). Your breakthrough could be right around the corner. Diligent work pays off and the Holy Spirit is with you to guide you and help you. Ask Him to reveal places where your mindset gets stuck and which verses or declarations to apply to your situation. Allow Holy Spirit to teach you what you specifically need for that season. He knows exactly how to work with you to get you to where you need to be. Whatever you do, don't give up.

A wise friend of mine said if we feel like we've been in the same season for a long time, then the only way to know if we are growing is by noticing how long it takes us to catch a bad thought or how much time we spend anxious and worried before turning to the Lord. I thought back over my life and realized that three years ago I would have responded to my current circumstances a lot differently than I did then now. If I had a deadline approaching and didn't have the money for it I would sit in anxiety weeks or months prior to the deadline until the money came through. I learned that I have a choice to answer the door to anxiety or leave the door closed. I realized that when it came down to the day something was due I no longer freaked out but was in total peace.

That is growth to me. You have to be able to look backwards and see how much you have grown and that will give you hope. I don't always recommend going into the past but I do believe in this instance it is actually very helpful to see just how far you have come.

When you review your journey of faith with the Lord, you can see just how faithful He has been and how He has never failed you. This is why I recommend again keeping a testimony book with you and writing down your financial testimonies, healings, or breakthroughs. Ask the Lord what He is highlighting in your season for you to record. For me it was finances. When you get into a place where you need a miracle and you need God to come through but you feel your faith wavering, you can go back and remember what He has done. Essentially, this is putting Philippians 4:8 into action. "Finally, brothers and sisters, whatever is true, whatever is noble, whatever is right, whatever is pure, whatever is lovely, whatever is admirable—if anything is excellent or praiseworthy—think about such things" (Philippians 4:8 NLT).

One day you will look back and realize that your mind truly has been transformed and that you no longer struggle with the same thinking patterns you used to have. Nothing is impossible with our God! Celebrate progress, not perfection. If it's just realizing one thought you have that produces fear or anxiety, celebrate that. You've just uncovered a lie!

COMPARISON IS DEADLY

Comparison is another common issue in our thought life but it stems from a deeper heart issue. Comparison is rooted in the orphan spirit. Speaker, Paul Manwaring, of Global Legacy describes the orphan spirit this way: "It says there is not enough. That it's not fair. Why is that person so favored and I am not?" God knows exactly what to give each one of His children. He knows what favor to put on each of His children for the specific season they are in and also what people need individually. Because we are the body of Christ, when one-person benefits and prospers, it benefits all of us. One person may get the breakthrough you've been praying for, how do you respond? A son or daughter celebrates another's breakthrough because they know that theirs is coming. A true son or daughter of God knows that there is more than enough to go around. An orphan spirit gets jealous, doesn't celebrate the other person, and doesn't see another person's success or breakthrough as fair.

Let's say you've been praying, interceding, and hoping for marriage for the last 10 years and then your friend who didn't even have marriage on her radar, calls to tell you she's getting married and you're still single. Do you truly celebrate with her knowing you can continue to hope in faith, or do you say, "That's not fair! She didn't even want to be married!" Out of the mouth the heart speaks. Situations will arise that will test the condition of your heart.

I currently reside in Northern California and have access to some of the most beautiful hiking trails that lead to stunning waterfalls and views of the Shasta and Trinity mountain ranges. The following vision made perfect sense to me because I hike quite frequently and could relate. I was comparing my life to someone else's the other day and thinking how different our lives were, yet parallel at the same time. I saw a mountain with two trails on it and the Lord said, "No two trails on all the earth are the same. Each trail is uniquely different. That's the beauty and adventure that comes with hiking." So why would we think our journey would be the same as anyone else's? We are all called to hike our own unique trail that leads to the same destination, to the heart of the Father. Not competing, not striving, not cutting others down but knowing who we are and being secure in our identity as sons and daughters.

I once heard a beautiful example from a friend of mine on keeping our eyes focused on our own calling. We are to keep our eyes focused in our own lane while holding hands of those next to us as we face forward, moving towards our destiny. This is what community should look like. Our eyes can be fixed on our own lanes as we spur one another on and hold the hands of our brothers and sisters in their lanes as we run together towards the same goal.

CHAPTER 5: SAYING YES TO JESUS

The nagging voice of fear and fear of other's opinions likes to play on repeat in your ear as you begin to voyage into the unknown and take risks of faith. I honestly think the fear of man is the primary deterrent the enemy uses to keep us from fulfilling our destinies and promises. I was recently on a walk with the Father, when Jesus reminded me that He went through everything that I'm going through and He understands what it feels like to have people think you're crazy or to be rejected and denied. Jesus is closer than a friend; He is the Emmanuel, God with us, our constant companion. He knows what it's like to go through hurt and pain. Jesus reminded me that even His closest friend, Peter, rejected and denied Him in the moment He needed him the most. Even Jesus had a need for deep friendships and community. Yet, in love and mercy, Jesus forgave Him. Peter even tried to convince Jesus to not go to the cross because he didn't understand God's plans. But Jesus knew the Father's plans and the joy set before Him was on the other side of the cross.

Even well-meaning people and Christian brothers and sisters may try to step in, convincing you to go in a different direction because they don't understand the plans of God for your life. In these moments you must trust your peace and the Holy Spirit within you. Even if people reject or are disappointed in you, Jesus knows exactly what that's like because He went through every form of human emotion during His ministry time on earth. You can always go to Him with every rejection, disappointment, fear, or hardship. He understands.

When Jesus asks you to step out and follow Him oftentimes your logic will try to come in and make sense of what He's asking you to do. But God works beyond our logic. His ways can't be neatly boxed up and tied with a ribbon. He likes to work outside of our paradigm.

Let's look at the story of Jesus dying on the cross. Think about this: Why wait three days after Jesus died to raise Him from the dead? Why the delay (to us)? Why the cross? Think about those who knew Jesus was the Messiah and the Savior. I'm sure they didn't think the Messiah was going to die on a cross. They thought He was going to be the King of the Jews, which He was, but not in the way they thought. Doubt, unbelief, and questions were probably going through their minds. But on that third day He rose victorious! History forever changed. In that day and time, they had to wait three days to officially pronounce someone dead. God knew what He was doing all along, even though it didn't make sense.

Sometimes saying *yes* to Jesus goes against everything in us that "wants" to say *yes*. But deep down there is a knowing that if I say *yes* to this, it's going to work out for the best, even if it doesn't make sense. In surrendering to Him, we find our destiny. He has only good things in store for us; and when we can allow this understanding to sink deep into our hearts, we are able to fully trust His ways.

There have been numerous times that I have tried to push forward with believing that God was moving but actually I was going against the current. I realized I was scared to give up full control and surrender to God. I said I trusted Him but deep down in my heart, I really didn't. *What if I don't get married? What if this is the only guy that will ever be interested in me? What if this means I will have no money? What if this is the best job opportunity I'll have?*

The more that you let go of control, the more you will see God come through in a mighty way. As in any relationship, the longer you walk with Him, the more you get to know His nature and character, and you'll be able to trust that He is faithful and trustworthy. Today may you encounter His nature and continue to grow to know Him so that you can learn to fully trust in Him.

WHO IS GOD TO YOU?

Who is God to you? Do you define Him by your experience or by what people around you are saying? Or do you base your definition off of what the Bible says about Him? Is God your healer, deliverer, provider, comforter, Father, and friend? Or do you view Him as angry, judgmental, out to get you, or not satisfied with you?

The Bible is the truth and the foundation of all truths, therefore, the way you view God must line up with who He is biblically. God sent Jesus to take all of our punishment and sin. Therefore, He is not waiting to punish you or release His wrath upon you. He did all of that through the cross. The verse in 1 John 4:18 differentiates fear and love, "There is no fear in love; but perfect love casts out fear, because fear involves punishment, and the one who fears is not perfected in love." The fear of being punished is because you do not have a full understanding of the love of God.

Throughout the Bible there are many different "names of God," which serve to give us a description of His character.

Throughout our lives God is revealing different sides of His face, known as His character. As you read over this list see which name is highlighted to you today and focus on that characteristic of God. Blue Letter Bible lists the following names of God (source #13):

- El Shaddai (Lord God Almighty)

- El Elyon (The Most High God)

- Adonai (Lord, Master)

- Yahweh (Lord, Jehovah)

- Jehovah Nissi (The Lord My Banner)

- Jehovah Raah (The Lord My Shepherd)

- Jehovah Rapha (The Lord That Heals)

- Jehovah Shammah (The Lord Is There)

- Jehovah Tsidkenu (The Lord Our Righteousness)

- Jehovah Mekoddishkem (The Lord Who Sanctifies You)

- El Olam (The Everlasting God)

- Elohim (God)

- Qanna (Jealous)

- Jehovah Jireh (The Lord Will Provide)

- Jehovah Shalom (The Lord Is Peace)

- Jehovah Sabaoth (The Lord of Hosts)

When you study the scripture the eyes of your spirit will be enlightened as you read and realize that God is good and He is not angry. He is kind and slow to anger. He is filled with compassion, mercy, and grace. Because Jesus bore the wrath of God on the cross you can have face-to-face friendship with God.

The enemy would want nothing more than for us to think that God is not actually good. The enemy is a professional at whispering lies in your ears. If you allow those lies to lead you, you come into agreement with the enemy.

Sometimes feelings come so strong that they feel like reality. Feelings aren't to be ignored but they can't always be trusted to lead your life. The Bible is meant to lead your life regardless of how you feel. Satan loves to skew our view of our circumstances and inject thoughts that challenge the very nature and character of God based on our experience. Especially when the natural circumstances are contradicting the nature of God, we have a choice to believe God or partner with the liar. This is when it is vital to know what scripture says about God's nature and to renew our minds to the truth.

Much of the church has formulated a belief that God is angry and judgmental and that He allows sickness and inflicts it upon people to teach them a lesson. I met a woman the other day that was in incredible pain and said, "I know God won't give us more than we can handle, but God this is too much." I thought, how silly does that sound? The one who allowed His beloved and perfect Son to die on the cross would inflict sickness and pain on us? That is a contradiction to what Jesus did on the cross. I too used to think that way until my mind was renewed. Bill Johnson often says, "A Kingdom divided will not stand. It's inconsistent to have Jesus pay a price for healing and for us to believe it's not God's intention to heal."

Once Jesus came as the kinsman redeemer He bore all sickness and took it to the grave with Him. Jesus' entire ministry was redeeming sin, sickness, and setting people free. He also challenged the natural mindset as He taught about the Kingdom. There are times in life when I can look at my circumstances and in that moment I have a choice to decide if

God is truly who He says He is or if I will let my circumstance define whether He is good or not. When my plans don't work out or hard times come, I can either get disappointed or remember that He works all things together for good. We live in a fallen world where there is suffering, pain, loss, and hardships. Staying in hope and choosing to believe for the best despite any circumstance shows real maturity. It shows you are grounded in the Word of God.

On the other hand, there is validity in expressing the pain in your heart and what you are going through with God and others around you who are a support. There is a difference between complaining and healthy processing. To war through life, and not give your heart a voice to speak, will end up doing more damage than good. So there is the tension of acknowledging the pain, sickness, problem, trial, tribulation, or hurt but landing in a place of hope.

You cannot forget that you are a citizen of Heaven. Citizens of countries have full access to what their country offers. **Since we are citizens of Heaven, we can access what Heaven has to offer us.** How do you do that? By training your brain through scripture and being aware of what you're meditating on. You can meditate on who God is and His nature with the following scriptures:

"The Lord is good, a strong refuge when trouble comes. He is close to those who trust in him" (Nahum 1:7 NLT).

"The Lord is slow to anger and filled with unfailing love, forgiving every kind of sin and rebellion" (Numbers 14:18 NLT).

"But God showed his great love for us by sending Christ to die for us while we were still sinners" (Romans 5:8 NLT).

"And we know that God causes everything to work together for the good of those who love God and are called according to His purpose for them. For God knew His people in advance, and he chose them to become like his Son, so that his Son would be the firstborn among many brothers and sisters. And having chosen them, he called them to come to him. And having called them, he gave them right standing with himself. And having given them right standing he gave them his glory" (Romans 8:28-32 NLT).

These verses reflect that God has unending, loyal love. He is not in a hurry to get angry but He is very patient with us. He even brought Jesus to die for us, as sacrificial love, while we were living in opposition to Him. God vulnerably gives people the ability to accept or reject Him. He also uses anything bad in our life and turns it around for good. Throughout the Bible, there is story after story of how God used evil for good.

Joseph stood on the conviction of his dreams even though he was captured and imprisoned, markedly far from obtaining his dreams. He knew that it was not God's nature to give him dreams and then not fulfill them. He knew that God was working out the bad for good, as stated in Genesis 50:20 (NLT:) "You intended to harm me, but God intended it all for good." Through the hardships of Joseph's life, God used that to promote him and launch him right into his dreams.

King David laments his soul to the Lord as he walks through the valley but he continues throughout the Psalms to draw on this one conclusion: God is good. "I will sing to the Lord because He is good to me" (Psalm 13:6 NLT). "You are my Master! Every good thing I have comes from you" (Psalm 16:2

NLT). The key is no matter what you face, no matter what opposition comes your way, no matter how bad or bleak things look, you have to land in a place of hope. The landing place of hope is that God is truly good and that no matter what you are going through, He works all things together for good.

Throughout Jesus' ministry here on earth, every person who was demonized, sick, or in sin, was completely healed and restored. Restoration is the purpose of the cross. Jesus' life demonstrated God's goodness and nature to heal every disease and sickness. Clearly, Jesus' entire ministry is a testimony of God's character. In Mark, Matthew, and Luke Jesus asked and answered, "Why do you call me good? Only God is truly good." Jesus knew the nature of His Father. That is why He was able to walk out in the authority and power that He carried because He knew His Father's character and nature.

Knowing God's nature and His plan for humanity to be restored to Him is what carried Jesus to the finished work of the cross. He knew the good plans God had in store for all past, present, and future humanity. Jesus could see the other side of the cross and the redemption, which is what enabled Him to carry out His assignment. "For the joy set before him, he endured the cross" (Hebrews 12:2 NIV).

We are called to carry the very likeness of Christ and become just like Jesus. The model Jesus gave us while He was on earth doing His ministry is the model we are to follow. By transforming our minds based on what scripture says about God's goodness, we will know Him. "Let the Spirit renew your thoughts and attitudes. Put on your new nature, created to be like God, truly righteous and holy" (Ephesians 4:23 NLT). As we allow the Spirit to renew our thoughts and attitudes we become like the One who created us. Through relationship and meditating on scripture you come to know God's nature and character, which makes it easier to say *yes* to His leadership in your life.

YOUR YES

One of my mentors once told me, "Figure out what your *yes* is and then your circumstances will line up. Don't look at your circumstances and allow them to dictate your *yes*." This piece of advice has stuck with me over the years. It's natural to want to look at your circumstances and say, "I don't have the money for that, this will never work out, or I'm not qualified to do that" but faith requires saying *yes* before every detail is worked out. As you begin to say *yes* to what's in front of you, you'll notice the ebb and flow of the next step being revealed at the right time.

At first it may take you a while to figure out which decision to make as you are learning to hear God's voice. In relationship you learn the ways the other person communicates, so is the same with God. Relationships are constantly growing and changing. That's the beauty of a relationship with God. As I continue to grow in my relationship with Jesus it has become easier to say *yes* because I know His faithfulness.

In our minds we think that the next step may have to look a certain way, but to God He has us doing something obscure and completely opposite to what we think it should look like. Nonetheless, it is the very thing that will lead us into the next step that we are supposed to take. It amazes me that you can be on the polar opposite end of the spectrum and yet you are actually closer to your destiny than you thought. You may be working at a random retail job that barely pays the bills thinking: *How is this equipping me for where I'm going? Or how is working at the coffee shop making lattes have anything to do with ministry?* Let me encourage you, it does. Every season of life is important.

I had no idea that working as a Subway manager was training grounds for future leadership. Like I mentioned earlier, before I was even saved I would come into work hung over but my boss saw the leadership calling on my life and promoted me to assistant manager before I ever thought I was worthy of such a position. I was put in charge of scheduling, employees, finances, closing and opening, and customer complaints. During that time I had no idea what that job had to do with what I wanted to do in life. All I knew was that it was a job and it was helping me pay bills and save for my future. That job was the beginning of me learning how to manage staff and conflict with customers.

Oftentimes we don't realize that what we're doing now is the next stair on the staircase for where we are going next. Whatever season you're in now is preparation for where you're going. God wastes nothing (1 Corinthians 15:58). Even the most obscure, miniscule parts of our lives, He uses.

GOOD, BETTER, BEST

You will be presented with opportunities and advancement that may seem good but are they the best? Once you are in the Kingdom, it is a matter of good, better, and best options. When you say *no* to the good you are saying *yes* to the best. God wants you to succeed even more than you do. As speaker, author and missionary, Heidi Baker, says, "God will not give the keys of a new truck to a 5-year old and say 'go have a drive'." That would be setting up that 5-year old for a disaster and a fatal accident. So why would He give you a platform before you're ready? He doesn't want you to quit, burn out, or have a major falling. He wants to promote you at the right time, when you're ready so that your character can sustain what He intends to give you. He's a good God and He is for us. His plans really are to prosper you and not harm you (Jeremiah 29:11). When He gives you a "no" on something, it is His protection, not punishment.

I met who I thought was my "ideal" guy; he fit everything on my list of what I wanted in a husband. After we had dated a few months I knew that he was not the one. I felt in my gut a "knowing" that Holy Spirit was saying "no" even though I kept trying to push past the red flags. I was angry with God because I felt like I was being punished. "Why God would you give me everything that I wanted in a man and then tell me no, he's not the one? That's mean! Why are you punishing me? I keep waiting and being faithful and I keep getting a 'no' and everyone else around me is getting married!"

Having a viewpoint like that clearly takes some time to work through, so those next few months were painful to say the least. I was bitter and upset with God. It wasn't until I could clearly see that God was so in love with me, and wanted the best for me, that He was actually protecting me, not punishing me. He knew that wasn't the man He had in store for me and to give me what I thought I wanted would actually be the unloving thing to do.

No matter how much I kicked and screamed God was holding me saying, "Trust me. I have the best in store for you. Just wait until you see who I have for you. He will make a more suitable spouse for someone else and so will you. You are going to be well pleased!"

Several years later it happened again. I met someone who I thought was ideal. I thought, surely this must be it! Because it'll take a miracle to find a man who has the same calling that I do. As time moved on I felt the same familiar pain in my back that I get when I know I'm off on something. I heard the same "no" I had heard a few years ago. This time I was even more frustrated because I started to hear the same lies *that I would never find someone, if I didn't say yes to this guy there wouldn't be another one, I'm only getting older and there are less single men the older you get.* You know, straight up, lies. Again God said, "Trust me, if I'm saying no to this, it's because I have the best in store for you."

God had someone who would make an even more compatible match in store for both of those guys and He has someone more compatible in store for me. This isn't just a one-way situation. He has the best in store for all people involved. God was once again protecting me, not punishing me. Once you begin to understand the true character of God, you can take any "no" that you get you and get excited because when you get a "yes", it is going to be the best.

Our greatest *yes* to Jesus is being faithful to what we currently have in front of us. I love dreaming and having vision, we need that to survive; but once you lose sight of your vision and stop dreaming, you stop living. However, how you handle your current assignment is also dependent on how you handle your next season. Imagine a line. At one end there you are and on the other end is your dream. They feel miles apart and it seems so distant. Your responsibility is not *how* you get to your dream, that's God's responsibility, your responsibility is to your current step.

Ask yourself, "What have I said *yes* to and am I being faithful to that *yes*?" If He has called you to change nations, then how are you being faithful to disciple the eight people He has given you? If you are called to own and operate a multi-million dollar industry with thousands of employees, then how

THE JOURNEY OF A RADICAL YES

are you doing with the four employees He has put under you?

"Whoever can be trusted with very little can also be trusted with much" (Luke 16:10 NIV). It's so easy to get caught up in the "how" of our dreams. *How am I going to get there? How will this all work out?* I have been guilty of this; being so focused on the future that I completely lose sight of the present and what I'm supposed to be getting out of my current season. Reset, focus your eyes on Jesus, and let all the "how's" fall off of you. As you keep your eyes focused on Him and continue to say *yes* to the thing that is in front of you, you'll eventually be walking in the midst of your dream. We will be living in the reality of what was once a far-off dream.

FINISHING WELL

One sunny winter day in Oklahoma, I was driving to work, passing through the brown fields that covered the majority of the state, when I saw a man. He was dressed in black from head to toe. He had an intimidating, really dark look about him; the type of guy you wouldn't randomly go up to. I knew I was supposed to stop and talk to him. As I pulled into the gas station, he was sitting on a curb with his head sunk low. I obeyed the Holy Spirit's prompting and walked up to him and said, "Hey sir, I wanted to stop and see if you're okay and if there's anything I can pray for you about." He responded, "I feel really sick and could use some Pepto-Bismol. Can you get me some from inside the gas station?" "Sure, I'll be right back," I replied.

As I came back walking towards the man, I gave him the bag with Pepto-Bismol and asked if I could pray for him. He said yes and I began praying that he would be healed. Then he pulled out his black tattered leather Bible and he asked if I could read him some scripture because he wasn't able to read it anymore because of his vision. I didn't expect that response; I guess he wasn't so scary after all!

I started thumbing through the Bible to pick a verse to read he alarmingly said, "Don't do that. Flipping around the Bible to find what you want to read. Just turn to the page the Holy Spirit is telling you to turn to." Shocked that I had just been scolded, I flipped randomly to Matthew 5. As soon as I started reading he started violently throwing up. I was caught off guard and wasn't sure if I should stop or keep reading. As I paused he said through throwing up "Keep reading!" Unsure of what to think of the current situation, I kept reading and he kept throwing up. As soon as he was finished he asked me, "Do you realize what just happened? Whatever was in my stomach couldn't stay in there once you started reading the Word of God, it had to come out."

Then he started preaching to me. "Don't you ever doubt your God. Do not doubt your God! Don't be like Moses who started out strong and then never made it to the Promised Land. So many people start off strong and never make it to their Promised Land. They begin doubting God and just like Moses, never get to enter the land they were promised," he said. Those words cut into my spirit like a sword.

He then proceeded to give me a rhinestone pin that said "Jesus" on it and wanted me to wear it. Reluctantly I put it on crookedly. He said, "No, put it straight and wear it like you're proud. That will make someone happy today." I fixed the pin and said goodbye to him and we parted ways. I never saw him again. That conversation has always stayed with me. I want to be someone who makes it to my Promised Land. I know that you do too. Say this with me out loud: "I will enter my Promised Land and I will take over the land God is giving me."

I don't want to start off fiery and then give up on my dreams and never make it to my Promised Land. I know that you don't either.

The ministry school I went to was flooded with people from all over the world that came to Redding, California on fire to see the world changed and know Jesus more deeply. It was easy to ride on the wave and momentum of the school. I knew that I had to keep my secret place with the Lord strong while using the momentum as an added tool. You have to fan your own flame. Concerts, conferences, preaching, podcasts, church, and community are all great things and they are the nutrients that feed our spirit but we can't dismiss our secret place with the Lord.

When I talk about the secret place I am talking about the time you spend listening to your Father's voice, communing with Him, engaging in conversation with Him, praying, and reading the Word. People who spend all of their time in the secret place and don't engage at church or with community become estranged. Equally, people who spend all of their time in community and letting others pour into them but never spend time in the secret place have not built a well deep enough to drink from during drier seasons.

When I meet with people one-on-one and they share that they're having some problems in a certain area and feeling disconnected from God, I have found it usually stems from not being in the Word. I'll ask them if they've been in the Word regularly and sure enough the answer is no. I think a lot of the problems we have can be solved from spending time in the Word of God consistently. Reading the Bible should always point us into a deeper relationship with God. Bill Johnson, often says, "We need both the Word of God and to experience the presence of God." I think all answers for every problem are found either in the Word of God, or in the secret place (being in His presence). That's where we get our identity from, affirmation of who we are, and instruction for our lives.

My most profound moments have come from the secret place when no one else is around. I can always tell when I haven't had enough time in the Word or the secret place. I feel the lack within me and the hunger and thirst to read the Word and encounter God being stirred up. I used to have a very regimented devotional time where I would have scripted out prayers that I would pray and a certain devotional book I would read. It was great for me to start out that way because I was developing a discipline in my life, but longevity wise it was becoming more of a religious routine. God would encounter me in those devotionals, but a time came when I needed to break away from my regiment and try some different ways of letting God encounter me.

Sometimes I would sit back and be silent. Other times I would pray and declare things out loud where I walk around and engage my whole body. Other times I want to read and write. Then there are times when I listen to worship music. Other times I'd go outside and take a walk, hike, or lie on a raft in the middle of a lake and not say a word. These are some of the different ways I encounter God. There is no formula. There is no box. Experiment with what works for you. Mornings tend to work best for me because it is quiet and still before the day starts. Plus, I love having coffee and sitting with Jesus in the mornings. For you, nights may work better. Figure out what works for you and make it a habit.

Just like a relationship, seasons change and the relationship takes on deeper stages. What worked for you in one season may not be what works for you in the next season. Some of my deepest moments have come from the simplicity of sitting in the sun allowing the warmth of the sun to encompass me while I am completely silent and not saying a word. I have found that when I go for walks in silence I walk away feeling so loved and known by God, even though we didn't exchange a word. We were just enjoying one another's presence. Sometimes during worship I like to sit back and be silent. I am so undone by the presence of God that I can't speak. Words don't do justice to what I'm feeling in my spirit.

My new favorite times with God have come out of complete silence because in that place I'm able to hear His voice so clearly. I can hear Him reaffirming me, reminding me of promises, speaking to my heart, and sharing His secrets with me. Silence used to irritate me because I felt like I needed to be doing something. Now I find it is something that I crave.

I go on Jesus dates every once in awhile where I take myself out to do things that I enjoy. This usually consists of some good coffee or a meal and then something outdoors. Today is Valentine's Day and I decided to take myself out. I went out for a coffee and some chocolate and then went to a beautiful park in town that is surrounded by several mountain ranges and filled with a few ponds. I sat back and let the sun warm me as I sat and reflected with Jesus on these past couple of years. I was overwhelmed with joy and thanksgiving as I thought about where He had brought me. He is so faithful to complete what He started. I didn't want to give much attention to what was next or any decisions that I needed to make. I just wanted to be with Him.

I remember the first time God told me to take the day and go on a date with Him. I was in a small lake town in Panajachel, Guatemala that has a phenomenal view of several volcanoes. I had lunch at one of my favorite restaurants in town and ordered a typical Guatemalan dessert, which is a plantain stuffed with black beans, chocolate and cream. I know it sounds weird but trust me it's delicious. I was the only person on the top level of the restaurant porch with a view that overlooked the lake. Talk about romantic; I loved it. Afterwards, I went to the pool and I felt so refreshed. I got to be alone with the One who created me, enjoying the things I love. God loves the things you love. What is it that you love? What makes you feel refreshed? Have you ever thought about inviting God into doing what you love and going on a "date" with Him?

Intimacy with God is what this life is all about. If you have intimacy with God you have everything. It is out of this place that you do everything else, not the other way around. He is more concerned with developing you as a person than He is about you reaching a watermark in ministry, or crusades, or how many attendees you have coming to service. Of course these things matter to Him, but the most important to Him is you heart. He cares more about our hearts than anything else. He wants intimacy and relationship with us, not a slave serving a master but a friend being a friend. We get to co-create with the Creator of the universe.

KEY INGREDIENTS

These are some of the fundamental "key ingredients" I have found that have helped me remain strong in this race we are called to live. First you have to get the foundational key; otherwise the others won't apply. The foundational key is the presence of God. Knowing that He is always with you. That He is not just with you, He is living inside of you. He has given you the Holy Spirit to be your counselor and guide, infusing you with power to do His will. Just like I talked about earlier with the story of the Israelites entering the Promised Land, God's presence was with them through the whole journey because they carried the Ark of the Covenant. They never departed from His presence. The key is seeking Him and abiding in Him. Apart from this place we can do nothing.

Jesus' life demonstrated abiding in the vine by the examples of how He drew His strength from the secret place. He did nothing that His Father in Heaven wasn't doing. So if we're seeking the presence of God and His Kingdom, then these other keys will naturally come into place. Striving for these keys does not produce any fruit. These keys are the overflow that comes from the secret place with God. God promised this in Matthew 6:33 (ESV) when He said, "But seek first the Kingdom of God and his righteousness, and all these things will be added to you."

Every great man and woman of God had a priority, and that was the secret place. Look at any person in history who did something great for God (Mother Theresa, Martin Luther King Jr., Billy Graham, Moses, Joshua, Jesus, just to name a few). All of them knew that their life was dependent on the secret place with God. It wasn't about their ministry or what they did for Him, even though they did amazing things for God, their focus was on their relationship with God. It was about them knowing their Father's business and getting those instructions in the quiet place and then going out to do the Father's business. From the secret place they had confidence in what God had called them to. No obstacle could stop them.

"The call of God burning in your breast will be uncontainable and unstoppable as you devote yourself to the fiery passion of intimate communion with the Lover of your soul" *Secrets of the Secret Place* by Bob Sorge (source #14). Those who prioritize the secret place, spending quiet time with

God, are propelled forward. They don't go to the secret place to advance their ministry but to feed their souls. The natural by-product of the secret place is fruitfulness.

If the enemy can distract us from the secret place by getting us busy doing our to-do lists, or thinking about all the other things we could be doing, or by over committing ourselves to activities, then he has us right where he wants us—weak and without strength because we are not abiding in the vine. It is wrong when we become so busy with activities that we miss the whole point, which is being with the Father. Every season is different and there will be other things that compete for our time with God but we have to make it a priority.

Now, let's look at some other keys for finishing strong. "Good leadership is built on love and truth, for kindness and integrity are what keep leaders in their position of trust" (Proverbs 20:28 The Passion Translation). I believe these four keys are vital to finishing well and they are also excellent values to build leadership upon.

Integrity is the first key ingredient to finishing strong. Integrity will always take you higher and open up more doors of opportunity. Opportunity will be knocking on your door if you build your integrity and character. Integrity is not something that can be imparted but something that has to be learned and developed internally. Doing what you say you're going to do is one way to build your integrity. If you don't know if you can commit to something, wait until you know if you can say yes or no. I used to over commit myself and then realized that I had committed myself to too many things. Some weeks I still look at my schedule and realize I over committed myself but for the most part, I'm able to really think things through before I make a commitment.

Paying your bills on time and developing your credit is

another way of building integrity. Managing your money, budgeting, not spending outside of your means are practical applications that you can build into your life. We live in quite the oxymoron right now. In this day and age integrity has lost its reverence, yet culture craves it and yearns for those who walk in integrity. Integrity also matters most when no one else is looking. How are you living your life?

Standing strong on your convictions is the second key to finishing strong. There are the obvious black and white answers that we can find in the Bible and then there is the gray area that the Bible doesn't address. For example, why is it that some people can watch certain movies while others feel convicted for watching that same movie? It may not make sense why you feel like you are the only one who can't watch a certain movie. Some may feel it's ok to listen to certain music, or have a drink and others will not. It all has to do with your calling and what is best for you as well as how it affects those around you and the people you're ministering to.

You may be put into a position of leadership where you have to follow a narrow path on behalf of the people who are following you so they don't stumble. Paul spoke about this in 1 Corinthians 10:23 (ESV): "All things are lawful, but not all things are helpful. All things are lawful, but not all things build up." The gray area of convictions is something that you will have to work out between you and the Lord. Everyone has different convictions about certain things that are not your "black and white" moral issues that the Bible addresses. Once you have those areas ironed out, you must stand strong on your convictions.

Much of the church today allows the world to impact the church causing the body to react, instead of the church impacting the world. Some Christians compromise their convictions for the ways of the world. They start to allow culture to shape their doctrine. There's also many people who talk about how dark and scary the world is getting and live in fear instead of being empowered to love in these dark times. We are called to be the light and should shine the brightest in the darkest of days. Instead of putting your focus on what you see as the current reality, let's get ahead of the game and speak out in faith what Heaven is doing. Ensure your conversations are hope filled and brimming with positivity. You have to use faith for what you do not see.

The world is looking for Christians who stand on their convictions but do so with love. You can love others without compromising; Jesus always did through His entire ministry (Romans 12:2). The body of Christ is called to change the world, and we have been given everything we need to do so.

"Look, I have given you authority over all the power of the enemy, and you can walk among snakes and scorpions and crush them. Nothing will injure you" (Luke 10:19 NLT). Now this verse has been taken literally and gotten a little wacky. I don't believe we are actually called to walk on snakes and crush a scorpion, that isn't using your brain. I believe this verse is used more figuratively as in we can trample and crush every demonic assignment under our feet because of the authority we have in Jesus. Jesus said that we would do greater works than He did.

Let's start believing what the Bible actually says and contend for more. We can go so much deeper in Him if we keep pursuing and pressing in for all that He has for us. The church should be the one influencing society, business, media, arts, education, technology, and healthcare. What stops us from doing so?

No matter what your circumstance is and how much you

are in need of a miracle, do not trade your convictions for something less than your calling. You are a child of God; therefore you are called to a higher standard of excellence. Live above reproach. Do not live substandard to your calling.

What do you do when you are the only person in a room that believes something the way you do? Have you built an internal system that will allow you to hold tight to your convictions without wavering because of peer pressure or fear of man? Sometimes you may be the only one with faith in a room and you have to decide not to listen to the opinion of man.

The third key to finishing strong is to be a trustworthy person. People around you need to know that you are the real deal—not out of a place of performance but out of a place of trust. Being who you are in every situation and circumstance builds trust. Being vulnerable and transparent creates safety and trust for those around you. People want to follow someone who is safe. It also allows other people freedom because they feel more at ease to be themselves when they are around someone who is genuine.

When people share secret areas of their life, do you keep it a secret or blurb it to someone else in the sake of a "prayer request" or needing to process? The more influence that you gain, the more people will open up to you and share vulnerable places of their heart. We want to be found as trustworthy, safe people. The best way to build trust is through love. When you truly love people and have no other agenda but to love them, trust will be formed. Trust coupled with an understanding, non-judgmental attitude is something the church needs right now. Again, this is not something that can be imparted. This is something that has to be built from the inside out.

We are royal sons and daughters of God (1 Peter 2:9).

Being that we are royalty and belong to a Kingdom, we must carry ourselves as royalty. Doing everything with excellence and to the best of your ability is Kingdom. I think the culture that we are in today has started to devalue character and we are at a crisis where we need people to not jeopardize their character and convictions for the sake of popular opinion. It will not always be easy.

Sometimes you will be the only one swimming upstream while a school of people swim by you going the opposite direction. You may be the only person to speak up on an issue when the entire room agrees on something entirely different. You must stand your ground. It is God's grace that gives you the power to stand strong in all of these areas. It is His grace that will empower you to build integrity, character, trustworthiness, and to stand your ground on your convictions. It is His grace that gives you the power to love others while not jeopardizing these areas.

Some of you will be put into the courts of kings and queens in governmental sectors and you must create an inner integrity, character, and boldness to speak the truth so that you are able to influence the influential. Strengthen your secret place with the Lord and you will not deviate or step away from what God has called you to. You must make Him the center of your everyday life, thoughts, and decisions. He wants to be invited into every area of your life.

The fourth and final key to finishing strong is surrender. Many people shudder when they hear that word. Especially those who love to plan, control, and know how things are going to look or workout before it happens. But we have been called to walk by faith and not by sight (2 Corinthians 5:7). This also means giving up our understanding or what makes sense to us. Once you know that God is good, surrendering will become easier for you. When you are unable to surrender, it usually stems from a root of control or a lie you believe about who God is. Surrendering is your greatest defense.

If I have learned anything this year, it's that God's ways are better than my ways. Combined with not having a job this year, and all of the changes that came with this year, I learned to let go of that last foot of rope that I was holding onto. God is so kind that He didn't ask me to give up the whole rope at once, but every year He has invited me deeper and has asked me to surrender more of the rope of control that I was so tightly clinging onto. As I have given up more control and surrendered to Him, I have come to know His character more deeply. I invite you to ask yourself today, "What area of my life do I need to give up control and surrender to God?"

CHAPTER 6: COURAGE IS NOT ABSENCE OF FEAR

As an American, I am surrounded by the pull to be comfortable. I am thankful to be a citizen of America and for the freedom won by those who came before us. But in America I see danger in getting too comfortable and relying too much on the accessibility of things we have at our fingertips. A lot of the structures and plans that America has in place seem to offer a sense of security. Not that these plans are bad, but they are not stable security. The only true security this world will ever find is in God.

The ground we walk on every day, the sun that rises every morning, and the moon that comes out at night are not as secure as the Lord, even though these things seem stable. In a world where things can change in a moment, you must find your stability and security in God alone. Nothing about the Bible promises safety and comfort. Actually, it promises the opposite. It promises that we will have trials and tribulations but to take heart because Jesus overcame the world. We can have unsurpassable peace in the midst of even the most chaotic, painful situation.

Bill Johnson always says, "You have power over the storm you can sleep in." Like Jesus, who was able to sleep in the storm and then commanded it to stop, we have also been given this same authority. No matter what God calls you to, you can trust in His peace wherever He takes you. I believe God is searching the earth for people who have great faith to trust Him and to follow Jesus wherever He goes.

If God is relational then we know He communicates with us. Don't be discouraged if you don't think you hear God's voice. I thought it was hard to hear His voice at one point in my life as well until I realized the ways that He speaks to us. He is always speaking through people, songs, movies, nature, animals, numbers, His Word, or from that internal "knowing" in your spirit. Those are just a few of the ways He speaks to us. He created everything; therefore His creation is always speaking to us. He is not silent, we just have to have eyes to see and ears to hear. It's figuring out the ways that God speaks to you that are key here. If you keep asking Him something and feel like He is silent on the matter, He more than likely already gave you the answer. Maybe you didn't like it or thought it was too impossible, but go back to the last thing you heard Him say.

When God speaks to you there will be times when those closest to you don't agree with what God calls you to do. There will also be times when He gives you contradicting words from people. Or you may hear contradicting messages (the message isn't wrong, it just doesn't apply to what God is currently teaching you). This again is to bring you into being completely dependent on Him. Just as the Bible has verses that seem to contradict themselves, it's meant to be read relationally. God is after our hearts. He will address one person very differently than the next person, depending on what the issue of the heart is.

There is wisdom in getting wise counsel and asking people around you for input, but I would highly recommend asking a select few trusted friends or people closest to you. When you get too many opinions you can feel like a ship at sea on a stormy night being tossed in several different directions. It is especially important to ask people who will not tell you what you want to hear, but will actually be able to be objective or disagree with you. This is also where your history with God comes in.

What has He asked you to do in the past? How have you seen Him come through and be faithful? What times did He ask you to do the impossible or move somewhere new and how did He come through for you before? Writing down testimonies and journaling is a good way to remember what God has done. When we get stuck between a "rock and a hard place" we often forget how faithful God has been to us. That's why having a journal, testimony book, sticky note reminders, or document on your phone is so valuable. You can pull it out and start reviewing God's faithfulness to build up your faith for the current task at hand.

My all time hero of faith is missionary, Brother Andrew. He was a missionary to closed nations where it was illegal to preach and have a Bible. The great exploits he did for the Lord and the extreme faith he had is so inspiring to me. One of my favorite books is *God's Smuggler*. Here Brother Andrew talks about making an illogical decision to attend a missionary school:

"Every reasonable sign seemed to point away from the school in Glasgow. And yet, unmistakable inside me, sublimely indifferent to every human and logical objection, was a little voice that seemed to say, 'Go'. It was the voice that had called to me in the wind, the voice that had told me to speak out in the factory, the voice that never made sense at a logical level" (source #15).

This is such a reassuring quote because the voice of God

often calls us to do something that doesn't make sense to our logical minds. Once you begin to walk with God long enough you know when you are walking in peace and when you have stepped out of peace. Even if God calls you to do something illogical but you have peace on it, trust yourself to follow Him. Trust that you hear the voice of the living God who lives inside of you.

Maybe courage does not come naturally to you; it didn't for me. Nelson Mandela, President of South Africa, said, "I learned that courage was not the absence of fear, but the triumph over it. The brave man is not he who does not feel afraid, but he who conquers that fear." Fear will be there but it's learning how to face the fear and get victory over it.

You may have to fight through the lies that tell you to be quiet, timid, and to hold yourself back because the reality is that timidity is not a fruit of the spirit. We are called to be bold, courageous, and free to be ourselves because the power of the living God is inside of us. Every person's battle looks different but one thing we can be assured of, we are not the first to experience what we are experiencing. Our brothers and sisters all over the world are experiencing the same battles (1 Peter 5:9). It is through God's power that we are able to be and do all He has called us to be.

Oftentimes, the very thing we are called to is the thing that we will experience the most fear around. For example, when I was a child I was quiet and didn't speak up much. When I was in middle school I would turn red if I was asked a question in class. I never wanted to raise my hand for fear of being embarrassed in front of the class. I was in such thick bondage to fear I could hardly function. My mind was a war zone filled with anxiety. I was entangled in the lies of the enemy and a prisoner to panic attacks.

As a child as well as in my early 20's, speaking up in class was quite the battle. The enemy had a hay day with that and would throw lies at me to keep me silenced in fear. My public speaking class in college was my greatest fear. I would completely freak out if I had to get up and present something in front of the class. I had to battle my thoughts every day and face every fear until I conquered it.

I remember as I prepared for the weekly meetings at one of my jobs and I would get in front of the mirror and look myself in the eyes as I grasped the edges of the counter in fear. I would speak directly to myself, saying how courageous I was and that I was going to speak with boldness. I would repeat, "I do not have a spirit of fear but power, love and a sound mind" relentlessly until I actually believed it. With sweaty palms and a quivering lip I would go into my meeting and face all 50 clients with whom I had to conduct a community meeting. I had to concentrate on breathing so that I wouldn't have to run out of the room in a full-blown panic attack. It wasn't easy, week after week I would get in front of that mirror and grasp the sides of the counter and look myself in the eyes and repeat scripture and declarations over myself.

But then, in time, something changed. I no longer was nervous speaking in front of groups and I didn't get nervous conducting the meeting. I began to realize that I was called to speak in front of people and the enemy had used fear to try and keep me quiet. That was only the beginning of the days I would speak in front of audiences. God found me faithful week after week renewing my mind to who I really was and what I was capable of. He didn't give me an easy way out but He was with me through every step of the way until I had complete victory in this area.

STEPPING OUT

I was doing my normal grocery shopping and while waiting in the checkout line when an elderly woman in front of me realized she didn't have her wallet. God prompted me to pay for her groceries but I thought to myself, *I can't do that. I don't have enough money for this week, plus I'll look stupid.* I'm being honest; these were the thoughts that went through my mind, like anyone would ever think someone was stupid for offering to pay for someone's groceries. It's crazy how much fear lies to us! She told the cashier to hold her groceries and she would go back home and come back to pay for them. I left the grocery store feeling like I had missed it. Thank God for grace because Jesus would give me plenty of opportunities from that day forward to step out. But I always remember this day significantly because I allowed the fear of not having enough money and what people thought of me to hold me back from blessing someone else. Fear will always tell you what you're not, what you don't have, and what you can't do. God is always whispering who you are, what you have, and what you can do.

When I first started learning about evangelizing I decided to start implementing it into my daily life. I was determined to make my everyday shopping a time when I could also minister to people. One time I was at Target in Norman, Oklahoma when I walked by a woman who I sensed was having terrible back pain. I was led to stop and pray for her. My initial thought again was: *I will look crazy. Was that really God? That was probably just me.*

I left the Target checkout line and headed to my car, but then I remembered my grocery store experience. "Ok, God. If that was really you, bring her by me again," I said. As I walked to the parking lot I realized I didn't remember where I had parked. I had to walk all the way back to the other side of the parking lot. Can you guess what happened next? As I walked to my car I passed by the same woman again. *This is God. I'm going for it!* I thought.

I walked up to her and introduced myself and asked her how her day was going. I asked if she had back pain and if I could pray and that she would be healed. She said she did have back pain and that I could pray for her. After I prayed she told me, "I had to leave Target because my back pain was getting so intense I could barely walk so I just decided to leave. Thank you so much for praying for me! All of my back pain is gone." I told her God loves her so much He healed her back. She said she went to church and knew God. As I said goodbye and walked away she got in her car and shouted to herself, "That was awesome!" I will never forget that day. I was beginning to recognize God's voice and when He was speaking to me.

I have had my fair share of rejection and people thinking I'm crazy for asking them if I can pray for them or being told, "The president is the one who really needs prayer, not me." The great thing about rejection is that it kills the fear of man. The more you step out and realize the authority you carry when you get rejected you won't allow that to jostle your identity or confidence. Knowing that God's love never changes is the antidote to rejection and fear of man.

WORDS OF KNOWLEDGE

Words of knowledge are simply asking God for specific things about the person. These can be phone numbers, addresses, pain in their body, birth dates, or dates of a significant event. This is a really powerful way to minister because it shows people how deeply God knows them that He would give a complete stranger something specific about their life and attach a word of encouragement to it. Several times I had tried getting words of knowledge and would get them wrong. There was even a point when I wanted to give up and thought: *I'm not gifted with that kind of prophetic gifting.*

I was in Bucaramanga, Colombia and was inspired by the team members and the way that some of them were walking in the words of knowledge gift. I thought *what the heck, I'll try it again* and I'm so glad I did. The Lord gave me a couple of specific dates for people during that trip down to the month, date, and year of a specific event in their life. From that place God gave me a word to encourage them. I have experienced this while going about my daily business and suddenly God will tell me something specific about someone.

Just the other day I was at a gas station in Oklahoma when I felt an overwhelming sense of compassion for the woman behind the register. God was telling me that she had two kids and she was an incredibly hard worker and she was stressed over some bills she had coming up. I felt so much compassion for her that when I started sharing what God was telling me I welled up with tears. I proceeded to ask her if she had children and when she said yes, I asked her if she had two. She pointed to one of them and said, "Yes, one of them is here helping me work." I told her what God had said and her whole demeanor changed. She said, "Oh my gosh, you have no idea! This helps me so much!" She looked more relaxed and was breathing deeper than before. I encouraged her that God loved her so much He sent a stranger, who didn't even know her, to tell her that. I blessed her finances and prayed for a breakthrough that all of her bills would be paid. It's really just that simple. You don't have to strive to share the love of God.

Ask God what He is saying about a person or situation and

He will answer you. Become aware of His presence and what He is doing as you go about daily life. You don't have to make evangelism and outreach an event but evangelism can be a lifestyle. As you go to buy groceries or get gas just tune in and become aware of what God is saying or doing. Oftentimes, we are so focused on our daily tasks, budgeting, and our list of what we need that we are completely oblivious to what God wants to do. I am not always aware of what God is doing but I am growing in becoming more and more aware. If I can hear God's voice like this, then so can you.

God longs to speak to you today. He wants to build you up and encourage you so that you can encourage those around you. We are His hands, feet, and mouthpiece. In a hurting world people are desperate to be encouraged and told they are loved and seen. Ask God what He thinks about the person you are interacting with and He will tell you how He created them and the great plans He has for them. "Without a vision the people perish" (Proverbs 29:18 NLT).

You are carrying the key and vision for some people's lives, take the risk and be God's mouthpiece. Someone's world can change today because of a word you give him or her. Start today by asking God: "God, please make me aware of your presence and what you're doing today in the people around me as I go out about my daily business. Let me hear your voice clearly."

A FIRE IN THE TURISMO BUS

It was a warm sunny day in Antigua, Guatemala as I waved goodbye to my friends at the mission house. The suspension squeaked as we were jostled inside the Turismo bus as it drove over the cobblestone streets. I always loved bus rides because

I would put in my earphones and reflect for a few hours on the trip, what God was doing in Guatemala, and what was coming next. I was headed to Guatemala City so with traffic, I had a good two to three hours on the bus.

I put my headphones in and sat back in my seat, as we started moving. The bus was filled with young people from all over the world and they were talking about how drunk they had gotten that week and how hung over they were feeling. I put my music playlist on pause to listen to their conversation when all of the sudden I felt this burning sensation hit my spirit. I felt compassion for these people and I could feel God's heart for them. They were lost and looking for purpose and fun, just like I used to do.

The more I listened the more I could barely contain the fire that was building up in my spirit. I knew I had to share Jesus with them. I sensed someone on the bus had pain in his or her heel so I interrupted the conversation to ask if anyone had heel pain. The bus fell silent and no one answered. So I regrouped and said to myself, "Ok, God. I'll try something else, but I know you are on this." I asked if anyone was in pain on the bus. A girl in the back answered and said she felt like someone had been sitting on her chest and she could not take a full breath. I asked if I could pray for her and she said yes, so I started praying and commanding whatever was making her chest tight to stop and to be at peace. She said she felt better but by the look in her eyes she was a little freaked out by what had just happened.

I explained to her about who Jesus is and how God still heals today. She began to tell me how she used to be religious but she walked away from God and was wondering if He would take her back. I told her of course He would take her back; His arms are wide open. All of this nonsense about God being angry and not loving is not who He really is. He is a loving Father and He waits with His arms open for us to come home to Him.

Then the guy on my right looked at me and said, "I've done some pretty messed up things in my life. Could God love me?" I told him the story about David and how God called David a man after His own heart. I told the bus my story and how God had changed my life and how much He loved them. That I too used to think getting drunk and partying was fun but life with Jesus was way more fun than that lifestyle ever was. I just couldn't say it enough, "God loves you guys so much! He isn't mad at you and His arms are wide open to you." After saying that a few times the conversation died down as we drove back to the city. When we got off the bus, the group of young people asked if I would have dinner with them, but I couldn't because I was headed to the airport. There was a man who had remained quiet the whole ride and pulled me aside and said, "Thank you so much for being courageous today. That was beautiful. God bless you."

You never know who you are on the bus with. You never know just how close someone is to coming back to Jesus. Or maybe they grew up knowing Him as a judgmental angry Father and their view of Him became skewed. Once they realize who God truly is they would want to come back to Him. The devil wants to keep people away from God by skewing their view of who He really is. You are His mouthpiece and there are people all around you who need to know about Him. Pray now that God would give you boldness and courage to go and share about Him to others. Pray that you will have a love encounter with God where you will be so madly in love that you can't stop talking about Him.

I have never regretted any risk I've taken. It always propels me into more growth and into stretching myself further than I thought. It also always punches fear in the face. We have been given such a vast inheritance as children of God and if we don't use it, it stays dormant and untouched.

I pray Ephesians 1:18 over you and that you may know the inheritance that is yours. "I pray that the eyes of your heart may be enlightened in order that you may know the hope to which he has called you, the riches of his glorious inheritance in his holy people" (Ephesians 1:18 NIV). Pour out what has been poured into you. Pouring out also makes room for more and gets rid of stagnancy or complacency.

In every season there are new ways that we can take risks. Pastor Banning Liebscher of Jesus Culture church said, "If you want to change the world, you're going to have to take risks." Everyone in the Bible who did something great that changed the world took risks.

AIRPLANE EVANGELISM

I was on a flight from Oklahoma City to San Francisco but had a layover in Denver, Colorado. I was talking to the Lord about how I wanted to keep adventuring with Him and taking risks; that I wanted to go out and proclaim His name to people and be sent out to the lost. A few minutes later I had a vision of me standing up on the airplane once we landed giving a very specific word about God's love. Instantly I felt the "fight or flight" response hit me and started thinking I was going to look crazy and possibly get dragged off the flight or have security called on me. But the more I contemplated following through a smile was brought to my face as I laughed knowing God was on this. The Lord being the sweet Father that He is said to me, "Christina, my love doesn't change for you whether you do this or not. My love stays the same." I smiled and thought how sweet He is. "There is a breakthrough in doing this if you want it." Well of course I wanted the break through.

The plane landed and we were on the tarmac for 15 minutes waiting for one of the portals to open. Once we got to the gate and everyone stood up to get their suitcases I knew it was a now or never moment. I knew in that moment, if I didn't do it, I would regret it. I felt this strong conviction in me that if I didn't say anything, then who would tell these people who my Father really is.

The fear was intense but I stood up and projected my voice as loud as I could, "Hey y'all excuse me." (You know being a southern girl has its perks in moments like these.) As I started to speak I could feel the power of God come over me. I felt tears welling up in my eyes and tried to get my emotions under control. Partially nerves and partially because I could feel God's Power surging through me as I spoke. But I knew this word needed to come out with all of my emotions. Through sobs I continued, "I felt very strong that there are several of you on this flight who think God is angry at you, or that He is a punishing God, or that you have done something to make Him angry but that is not Him. He is a God of love and He loves you guys. I don't know who that is on this flight but I felt strongly it's a few of you. I bless you guys to come to know His love and to know Him. Thank you guys!" Then I sat down trembling because of the mix of emotions and the fact that I did the thing that scared me the most.

I felt prompted to do this one other time on a plane and I didn't do it because I was so terrified. But this time I did it, still afraid but I did it. I got a mix of responses from people rolling their eyes, to looking away from me, while some were glued to every word I was speaking. I had a couple quietly say "thank you" to me and another lady grabbed me after the flight and thanked me for being so courageous. I knew in that moment that I was being obedient, regardless of the outcome, and that the people who heard it had the opportunity to hear about God's love for them. The crazy part is, no flight attendant said anything or came to remove me.

I share these stories with you because I want you to know that you can do this too. It doesn't have to look like getting on an airplane and "open air preaching" for you, but don't let fear keep you back from sharing God's love with those around you. The Holy Spirit will empower you with boldness and the right words to speak. Even if you are feeling fear, do it anyways! God wants to empower you to be His voice to His lost children. Nothing is impossible for you! Remember, I was the girl who would blush when she spoke in public. I would cower in large groups and suffered from panic attacks. Now, I may feel fear but I know the risk is worth stepping out and it is the Holy Spirit working through me. Take risks. Do the things that scare you the most. Courage grows when we do the things we are afraid of.

CHAPTER 7: SPREADING THE KINGDOM

Once you say *yes* to Jesus, you have been given a mandate to spread the Kingdom. As a son and daughter of God, you no longer live life just for you; you become "others" focused. In whatever area you are called to, you have influence to spread the Kingdom there. The Gospel is meant to be contagious, like a wild fire that rips through a forest and cannot be stopped. The entire Bible is based on the spreading of God's Kingdom but the real turning point is the start of Jesus' ministry. After He is crucified and resurrected the Gospel begins to spread with intensity because of the Holy Spirit coming upon the disciples. Once the Holy Spirit is deposited into the disciples in Acts 2, they are filled with power, boldness, and confidence to preach the Gospel.

The power of the Holy Spirit is still available for you today. You can be filled with the same power, boldness, and confidence that were written in Acts 2. The power of the Holy Spirit is meant to change the world. Even if you are in a place right now where you don't feel bold and courageous, don't despair; the Holy Spirit is here to help you.

PETER'S JOURNEY TO BOLDNESS

Becoming more bold and courageous can be a journey, just like it was for Peter. Because of fear, Peter denied Jesus three times on the night Jesus was taken from the Garden. In Luke 22:61 (NLT), Peter remembers what the Lord had said when he denies Him the third time. Suddenly, the Lord's words flashed through Peter's mind: "Before the rooster crows tomorrow morning, you will deny three times that you even know me. And Peter left the courtyard, weeping bitterly." Peter denies Jesus three times just like He said he would. But in Acts 2 we see that Peter becomes one of the boldest, most courageous of the disciples because he is filled with the Holy Spirit. He went from being afraid of man's opinions to boldly preaching the Gospel. He was the first one to speak up about what was happening when the disciples were filled with the Holy Spirit (Acts 2:14-15).

No matter how timid or insecure you may feel right now, God can come on you in a mighty way, and through the Holy Spirit empower you and fill you with courage. It wasn't until persecution hit the disciples that we see them taking the Kingdom out from Jerusalem. "The members of the council were amazed when they saw the boldness of Peter and John, for they could see that they were ordinary men with no special training in the Scriptures. They also recognized them as men who had been with Jesus" (Acts 4:13 NLT). People recognized that these same men who fled and ran in fear the night Jesus was crucified were now boldly teaching the scriptures, and they were amazed.

THE MAN ON THE OTHER SIDE OF THE STEEL DOOR

Coming into the understanding of the authority that I carry has been a journey for me. The stories that I shared in the previous chapter were the byproduct of the journey I went on in regards to the authority that I carried. It didn't happen overnight.

When I lived in Chichicastenango I could see the heavy influence of the demonic that sat over that region. There was a lot of witchcraft and witch doctors that had a strong influence on the area. I was actually scared at one point by how much darkness I saw. There was a man who lived in the town garbage dump, and once the dump closed he moved to the graveyard. The people of the town treated him like an animal; it was really sad. He walked around out of his mind most of the time and I would say he was demon possessed.

One day I was sitting on the curb in front of the ministry house in the center of town talking with one of the local boys. When I turned back to look at the little boy, he had taken off and I wasn't sure where he went. Then I looked up and saw that the man who lived in the graveyard was B-lining it right at me. I had just enough time to jump up and run inside the threshold of the door and turn around to try and shut the steel door. As I put all of my body weight into trying to shut the door, the man was on the other side screaming in a language that was not Spanish or Quiche. It literally sounded like a monster. He was very strong and he kept trying to push the door back. With one final slam, I slammed my body against the door and it shut and locked. My heart was racing; I felt like I was going to pass out.

I let a huge sigh of relief out and walked to the back of the courtyard and went into the mission house. Some of my co-workers were asking me if I was okay because I'm sure my eyes said it all. I explained the situation to them and then calmed down enough to take a tuk tuk back to the ministry compound where I was staying.

From that day forward I was so afraid of running into that

man again. I was wrapped up in a cocoon of fear over what would happen if I saw him again. Whenever I headed into town by myself I was always looking over my shoulder in hopes that I wouldn't see him again. A wave of fear would come over me every time I had to walk into town by myself. I didn't know what I would do if I came face-to-face with him like that again.

I was waiting for my co-workers one day in the truck while they were inside the ministry house. I looked in the side mirror and saw the same man that I was terrified of was going to be walking right by the truck. I freaked out and lowered my seat all the way backwards so that he wouldn't see me when he walked by. The windows were darkly tinted and I figured if I lay as still as possible he wouldn't see me. I locked the doors and froze. After he passed by I let out a sigh of relief. I knew deep down I shouldn't have been afraid of him but I didn't understand the authority that I carried.

Then, one day as I was walking into town, covered in a wave of fear, the Lord said to me, "Christina, why are you afraid of that man? Greater is He who is in you than he who is in the world. Do not fear that man, he is my child but he is a captive in darkness." My heart changed towards the situation as I saw that man as one of God's children, who were being tormented and that wasn't okay with me. No longer would I walk in fear of darkness but I was able to have eyes to see that all people are God's children and those who are possessed by the enemy are held in the captivity and torment by the evil one. From that day on I knew that no matter what, God was with me and that I did not have to live in fear of the demonic.

Now, years later, I can look back at that situation and how I would've handled it differently. I understand now the authority that I carry and I look back at that situation and see myself holding my ground, not running, and not living in fear. That man had some evil spirits with him that he needed freedom from but he was an inflicted man made after God's own image.

As you spread the Kingdom you will encounter darkness. A missionary in Colombia told me once that he asked God, "God why am I seeing so much opposition in my life right now?" God answered, "This is actually a good sign because you are taking over more ground and pushing the darkness out. This opposition you feel is the light bumping into darkness and driving it out." What a great way to look at why we experience opposition. Especially, as we advance the Kingdom and take on more territory there can be more opposition. As Kris Vallotton, Senior Associate Leader of Bethel Church, says, "New levels, new devils." Of course this is not meant to produce fear, but that you would realize the magnitude of the spiritual war we are in.

Much of the church either lives in complete silence or ignorance of the darkness, pretending it doesn't exist or they're scared of it and don't know how to handle it. The church must wake up to the reality of the war that is going on around us. Once we became followers of Jesus Christ, we enlisted in God's war. Jesus has given us *all* authority over *all* evil (Luke 10:19). I don't live being devil-focused, I stay God-focused. But I don't ignore the battle going on around me and I have been confronted by the demonic, so I know it is real. Demons like to put on a facade that looks scarier than they really are.

The Christian who realizes that he/she has authority over the demonic is the one all of Hell is afraid of. When you are confronted with a person who is demon possessed, remember, love conquers all. I have heard crazy stories of people who scream at demon-possessed people, have them throw up in buckets, and make a big ordeal out of it. Satan doesn't deserve that much glorification. Simply love the person, because they are a child of God and with authority cast the demon out in Jesus name. You may have to do it more than once but remember—you have the Holy Spirit. Listen to Him on how to handle the situation. Holy Spirit will guide you in exactly what you need to do to get the person free. But always be in a place of love and remember there is a real human being, a child of God behind the facade of scariness.

NO REASON TO FEAR

Once you know that you are loved and the fullness of your identity, there is no reason to fear. Jesus knew His identity and His calling and let nothing waiver or detour the reason He was on the earth. He made a way for all of us to collectively spread God's Kingdom together. In Matthew 6:33 (NLT) Jesus says to "Seek the Kingdom of God above all else, and live righteously and he will give you everything you need."

Jesus' life was an example of how He was only about His Father's business and He always kept His eyes, mind, heart, and ears on what God was doing. He was focused on His Father and His Father was focused on Him. He kept the Kingdom of God the main thing and everything else flowed from that place. His entire ministry of healings, signs, and wonders were from a place of keeping God's Kingdom above any other thing. Matthew 6:33 is an instruction to us on how to live our lives. When we fill our lives with the cares of the world, it drags us down and hinders our focus, but when we prioritize the Kingdom as the main thing, everything else falls into place.

EVANGELISM

Evangelism can be a word that tends to send people running. The misconception of evangelism is that people believe only certain people are called to evangelize, when in actuality, we are all called to evangelize. Evangelism looks different for every person and it can have your unique personality and twist on it. I'll go over this in more detail below.

In Mark 4:13-20, Jesus uses a parable to teach on how the farmer plants seed by taking God's Word to others. He explains how some seed fell on good soil and other seed did not make it into the soil because it got choked by the cares and worries of life, some seed did not have deep roots, and other seed fell away because of persecution. But the good seed accepted the Word of God and produced 30, 60, and 100 times as much as had been planted. Here we see how it works when we take the Word of God to others and how there is a huge harvest that comes from sharing the Word of God.

The thing about evangelism is that it doesn't have to look like the way anyone else does evangelism. Some people will evangelize with fire and power, which may look more loud and outspoken. Others will approach evangelism through acts of kindness or love. Both forms are done based on love. Buying someone's coffee, smiling at them, acknowledging someone or encouraging them are all forms of evangelism because the living God inside of you is coming out through these gestures. Therefore, people are encountering God because of your presence. I actually believe that you can look into someone's eyes and they can encounter God because He lives inside of you. As they look into your eyes, they are looking into Jesus' eyes.

One of the most powerful encounters I had with this was when I was in Cambodia at an orphanage. I held this beautiful little girl's face in my hands and looked into her eyes. I could feel the love of Jesus pouring out of my eyes and looking into hers. We both started crying as I held her face and wiped her tears away. We didn't speak the same language and I don't know what God was doing in that moment but it was more powerful than any word I could've said. We both walked away from that encounter touched by God's immense love.

I actually believe that there is a time and place for each form of evangelism. Like the story earlier about the tourismo bus, I felt a literal power and fire come over me to share the Gospel the way that I did. Other times it looks like meeting a simple need or being kind. Then there are times I'm not suppose to do anything at all but let my mere presence change the atmosphere. I can walk into any place and just by me being there the atmosphere changes because the living God is inside of me. Evangelism is to be done with Holy Spirit. He will guide you as you navigate how to share the Gospel and in what way. As you ask for God's heart for the person you are ministering to and for the Holy Spirit to guide you, He will show you the best way to evangelize to that person.

Advancing the Kingdom of God does not mean that we have to strive to advance His Kingdom. There are so many different ways to advance the Kingdom of God. What are some ways you can spread the Kingdom in your work place, family, and city?

OUR DUTY

As an ambassador of Christ you have the responsibility of the farmer, to spread the seed (the Gospel) throughout the world. When the seed spreads, individuals have free will to choose what they will do with the seed and how they will respond. May you be a person where the seed goes deep within you and becomes a 30-, 60-, or 100-fold harvest. Don't let concerns, worries of life, offense, disappointment or persecution cause you to give up and not finish the race.

It is easy to be persuaded to stay comfortable and not allow the Kingdom to really take hold of you. You can fill your life with things, people, and comforts instead of allowing yourself to be uncomfortable and inconvenienced to spread the Gospel. When times get hard or there is persecution, some people decide it is not worth continuing to walk with the Lord. It breaks my heart to think of that because the trials of this life are temporary and what is coming is so much greater than we can imagine. You have to keep your perspective fixed on Heaven because that is eternal, while the hardships of life are temporary.

Something I learned a while back was that I needed to live like I was on the mission field everyday. When I stopped living from a place of "once I arrive there, then I'll do this" and started doing it now, it was a lot easier to share the Gospel and spread the Kingdom when I did go on missions and ministry trips. Even in the simple, mundane things, you can release the Kingdom of Heaven.

Remember, wherever you go, darkness has to flee because the living God lives inside of you. Pay attention today how you can love someone. Even if it's just one person a day, start today. Ask God how He wants to love the person in front of you, through you!

CHAPTER 8: BREAKTHROUGH

Breakthrough is a term used to describe a sudden change in a situation or person's life. Throughout this chapter I am going to go through some practical ways that people experience breakthrough as well as the sacrifices it takes for your situation to change. For example, there's an area you've been praying and contending for; perhaps for health, to see a family member saved, marriage, kids, etc., when suddenly your situation changes and the answer comes. Everything changes for the best and life is no longer the same as it was yesterday. God is the God of breakthrough. In an instant, He can break through and change any situation. Sometimes breakthrough is a process as God is rewiring the way you think and respond to situations and sometimes breakthrough happens suddenly.

HOW TO GET BREAKTHROUGH

Breakthrough must be sown with prayers of intercession. Praying is crucial if you want to see change in your life. Get into the secret place and pour out your heart to your Father. You can pray throughout the day, while you are doing the dishes, driving, or walking. Prayer can be a constant all-day dialogue with the Lord. Make your requests known to the Lord and then thank Him for what He has done.

Thanksgiving opens the gateways to breakthrough. "Enter

his gates with thanksgiving and his courts with praise; give thanks to him and praise his name" (Psalm 100:4 NLT). Bill Johnson, always says, "Thank God in advance as if it has already been done. Celebrate the miracle before it happens." I felt odd at first as I began to grow in celebrating my miracles before they would happen, but then something would happen. I could feel faith igniting and my hope being lifted as I started to thank God for what He was doing before I could see it.

I would thank Him, "God, thank you for the way you are going to pay my rent. I don't see how but you do, thank you for the way you are going to provide for me. God, thank you that you know I need a job and finances to pay my bills. Thank you for bringing me jobs this week. God, thank you for the way you are going to feed me today. God, thank you, you know that I need a car, and I thank you for the way you are going to provide one." Sure enough, He always came through. I would feel anxious when I would look at my circumstance but peace would flood my heart as soon as I started thanking Him for providing for me. He always provided. Praying this way brings you out of a spirit of fear and into the spirit of faith.

TITHING & GENEROSITY

Another area of breakthrough is through living a lifestyle of generosity and tithing. Tithing and generosity are an act of worship to God. These acts have a cause and effect principle. "Give, and it shall be given unto you: good measure, pressed down, shaken together, and running over will be put into your bosom. For with the same measure you use, it will be measured back to you" (Luke 6:38 NKJV). This is the one area in the Bible in which God says it's okay to test Him.

"'Bring all the tithes into the storehouse so there will be

enough food in my Temple. If you do,' says the Lord of Heaven's Armies, 'I will open the windows of Heaven for you. I will pour out a blessing so great you won't have enough room to take it in! Try it! Put me to the test! Your crops will be abundant, for I will guard them from the insects and disease. Your grapes will not fall from the vine before they are ripe,' says the Lord of Heaven's Armies" (Malachi 3: 10-11 NLT).

When you are experiencing lack, it's a great time to give. When you are generous with little, you will be entrusted with much. It is the exact opposite way to live in the natural; if you don't have enough you wouldn't give it away. However, we are called to give even in our greatest time of need. If you feel like money has a hold on you, start giving it away and that will break any grip that money has over you. It is imperative that you are tithing your income. I can't stress the importance of this enough. When we are faithful to tithe what God has given to us, we never know what we are sowing into down the road.

A tithe is the first 10% of your income, which comes from Deuteronomy 14:22 (The Message Translation), "Make an offering of ten percent, a tithe, of all the produce that grows in your fields year after year." If you want to give above and beyond that, do it! As Brother Andrew says in his book *God's Smuggler*, "We stuck fast to two rules: we never mentioned a need aloud and we gave away a tithe of whatever came to us as soon as we got it" (source #16). God always came through for Brother Andrew and He will come through for you.

This principle is set in stone. Give and it will be given to you (Luke 6:38). I have seen this principle work for people who don't even believe God exists, yet they are more generous than some Christians I know and their business are blessed and flourishing because of it.

On a missions trip to Cambodia our mission team ate lunch

at an amazing restaurant in the city of Phnom Penh. We liked it so much that a group of us went back for dinner. As I got to talk with the owner I noticed that his business was built on excellence. If you didn't like the food, you could send it back with no questions asked and they wouldn't charge you for the meal. The owner even said if you ate half of it and decided you didn't like it, they'd get you something else without asking questions, free of charge. He then went on to tell us the story of how his restaurant came about. He was a very wealthy man who owned a multi-million dollar business and he had flown all over the world. He came to Cambodia and realized all of his wealth and belongings meant nothing, especially compared to the brokenness and poverty he saw there.

He met a woman who was working at a gas station earning $20 a week and she cooked a meal for him. He said it was one of the most amazing meals he'd ever had. He told her she was wasting her talent pumping gas and needed to be cooking, so he promised to open a restaurant, where she could cook and earn money for it. He gave up his wealthy lifestyle to open up this little restaurant in Phnom Penh, and named it "to waste your talent," in the Khmer language. The woman became the head chef and co-owner of this restaurant.

The restaurant has become very popular and is doing quite well. He centers the restaurant on family; and the employees look out for each other like a family. If that is not amazing enough every night they take the extra food or the food that people returned down to the river to feed the homeless. He asked the surrounding restaurants to join in and even offered to take their extra food for them, but they declined. And you know what the kicker is? He said he's an atheist.

SACRIFICIAL GENEROSITY

Another level of generosity is sacrificial generosity, or generosity that comes with a cost—"give until it hurts." I have seen this put into action more in third world countries where people have nothing, yet they are incredibly generous and it is tremendously humbling. My team and I were walking down a dirt path to visit a family that lived at the bottom of a hill in the rural mountains of Quiche, Guatemala. As we walked through the cornfields we could smell the smoke from a wood-burning stove as we got closer to the house.

When we arrived we were greeted by a large toothless smile and told to come into the house. The entrance was so small I had to duck to not hit my head on the doorway. We sat on the dusty ground as this sweet widowed grandmother began talking to my co-worker. She was raising her two grandchildren by herself and was only making $1 a day by selling things at the market.

As the visit went on she took the corn she was boiling off of the stove and gave us three huge ears of corn. I was shocked by this woman's generosity. That was her family's lunch, yet she gave us her best and largest produce. We had brought fully packed lunches with us that day but to turn down her generosity would have been rude. That corn cost her something; that is radical generosity.

On a gray, rainy day during wet season we made our way down the steep slick paths in a rural town outside of Chichicastenango to a group of houses where a family lived. There were no men in this family, just women and children. The kids were running around barefoot as they saw us come down the hill and ran inside to get their mothers. The mothers of the family made a small amount of money from selling hand-made articles that they sold in the market. Once we arrived they greeted us with an oatmeal drink, some crackers, and a bag full of fruit. Again, I was astounded by the generosity of this family that had little to nothing yet lavished us with food. This became more of a norm. Several families we visited showered us with generosity. These are just some of the many stories I have seen that have completely wrecked me and challenged me to be more generous.

What is God challenging you to give? Is there someone or something He is asking you to sow into? Could the breakthrough you need be found in sowing into someone else?

LAYING DOWN YOUR DREAMS FOR A SEASON

After I knew the Lord had called me to Guatemala, I felt like I had to go right away. When someone prophesied over me about going, I didn't understand that it meant I had a long journey in front of me to bring me to a place where God could use me to change a nation. Every time I left Guatemala to come back to the United States I felt like a piece of my heart was being ripped out. I always cried the whole way back home as my heart was breaking all over again. I had never experienced anything like that for any other nation or anything else in my life. Once I started ministry school I knew God was equipping me for something so much bigger than I could even imagine.

I finally came to the place where I surrendered my desire to go and I laid it down at the Lord's feet. I simply prayed, "Jesus, I know this dream is yours and that you are the One who gave it to me. You want to see it happen, even more than I do. I know you will pick it up when the time is right."

Laying down your dreams is easier once you know God's character. It requires knowing that you can trust Him and put your faith in Him. Ultimately every dream is His and He wants to see it come forth even more than we do. He knows the right timing, people, and provisions so that dreams can be birthed in fruition. Timing is key. He is so loving and kind that He will get us ready for what He has called us to.

For example, if you are called to change a nation, God has to get you and that nation prepared so that both will be ready at the same time for what He has in store. There are businesses, creations, songs, stories, books, films, medicine, and cures that have yet to be created. Right now, you are carrying dreams inside of you that need to be birthed in the right season.

God is so kind and good that when He asks you to give up a dream it's because He wants to produce the character and integrity that can hold the weight of the calling and blessing He wants to give you. He would rather you go through a hidden season of character building that sets you up for success, rather than to see you walking out your dream before it's time. Scripture states that the gifts of God are irrevocable (Romans 11:29).

I believe that we can see this a lot in Hollywood. So many actors and actresses have amazing gifts but their character and integrity were never developed before they got a platform, and they end up having an ugly fall. The platform can kill if character isn't the solid foundation that the platform is built upon. Your breakthrough is often found in surrender and allowing the formation seasons to take place.

I have heard countless stories of well-educated people who were very successful that felt led to drop everything for what God was calling them to. They worked at jobs they were over qualified for, that paid less and cleaned toilets, or did janitorial services at the church. In these seasons the Lord was working on their character and humility. At the right time they were exalted, and now they have amazing platforms and are in leadership positions changing the world.

The end result is not about being in leadership, it's about being the best at what you are called to do. If you are called to be a husband or wife, then allow God to build your character to be the best husband or wife you can be. Your marriage can change the world. People need to see living examples of healthy marriages. If you are called to be a musician, then allow God to build your skills and character so that you can create and write music that will change the world. If you are called to be a mother, allow God to build your skills and character so that you can raise world-changers. Raising children is no small thing. You are raising children to know the Lord and His ways. Whatever you are called to, do it excellently, and allow God to do the building work within you.

PLACING YOUR DREAMS ON THE ALTAR

Abraham experienced breakthrough in his life by obeying God's request and surrendering to what God was saying, even though it made no sense. Abraham was given a promise from God that He would be the father of many nations and that his descendants would outnumber the stars. Then in Genesis 22 God tested Abraham's faith. He told him to take his only son and sacrifice him on the altar. This story fascinates me because just a few years prior, God had given Abraham this great promise and now he was asking him to set his promise on the altar and offer his son as a burnt sacrifice.

God was testing Abraham's heart and if he truly believed what God had spoken over his life. I believe Abraham had a deep understanding of the nature of God and he knew God would provide a sacrifice in place of Isaac as he headed up the mountain. You can see this in Genesis 22: 7-8 (NLT) in the dialogue between Abraham and Isaac.

"Isaac turned to Abraham and said, 'Father?' 'Yes, my son?' Abraham replied. 'We have the fire and the wood,' the boy said, 'but where is the sheep for the burnt offering?' 'God will provide a sheep for the burnt offering, my son.' Abraham answered. And they both walked on together."

It is almost as if this strange request did not even shake Abraham. Sure enough, God provided a ram and Abraham sacrificed it to the Lord and named the place Yahweh Yireh, that means, "the Lord will provide."

Is God calling you to lay down your dream? When God asks you to give up a dream, He always returns it to you 100-fold and 100 times bigger and better than you thought.

When God asks you to lay down your dreams, it is not because He is a mean God, but it is His kindness. He either wants to work out the things in you that can't stand for where He is taking you or He has something so much better in store for you than you realize. He is after your heart. The more you come to know God, the easier it is to lay down your dreams because you know He is truly a kind God.

For you singles who sought God's heart on the relationship and He said no, let me reassure you; He is still bringing you the best spouse. His "no" on a relationship is His protection. If He is saying "no" to someone you are dating, it's because He has the best in store for you. He has someone who will compliment you perfectly. Someone you will be equally yoked with. The enemy will try to come in and tell you that you will miss your chance or there won't be another opportunity or person like the one you are with now. But those are lies to keep you from experiencing the best God has for you.

WALKING IN THE REALITY OF A DREAM

It was a last minute decision to drive down to Waco, Texas while I was in Dallas visiting a friend of mine. Spontaneous trips are my favorite. We went to visit Chip and Joanna Gaines' Magnolia Market from the TV show, *Fixer Upper*. It was the middle of December but the humid warm air from the Gulf of Mexico blew through the marketplace making it feel as if it were a beautiful summer day. I was thankful for some warm weather but definitely did not pack for such a warm day. I was literally sweating in my boots.

As I walked around the market I could feel the pleasure of the Lord. He loved what Chip and Joanna were doing. I love their story because it attests to laying down your dreams and the faithfulness of God to pick them up in due time and breathe life on them again. You can read their full story in their book *The Magnolia Story* and how Joanna had laid down her dreams for a season to raise her children at home.

Years later the Lord reminded her of her dream and said it was time to pick it back up. She wrestled through picking the dream back up but she eventually did. Suddenly, the Gaines' lives changed and they experienced breakthrough in their lives. God breathed on the dream with favor beyond anything they could have ever imagined.

Their business is booming and it keeps growing. Now they own a plot in the downtown district of Waco. The online store and Magnolia Market is there, they have a bakery, fun area for families to play together, and food. As I walked into the home goods store the Lord said, "Christina, you are walking in the reality of a dream. This was once a dream for them and now it's their reality. They haven't reached the lid of their dream; it will keep growing. This is what it looks like to dream big."

This story really speaks to me because it shows me what God does with a dream that is laid down. He picks it back up, breathes on it, puts favor on it, and it takes off. It becomes bigger than we could have ever imagined. Just yesterday, the Gaines announced their new line that is available at Target. Their dream continues to grow and we haven't seen the fullness of everything they will do.

All of these stories show the different ways that people laid down their dreams as they continued to say *yes* to whatever season God ordained in their lives. They allowed God to do what He needed to do in their hearts. Of course, this isn't always easy; sometimes we come out of these seasons with a limp from wrestling. But the beauty of these stories is the redemption and how God suddenly broke through their situations and how it changed history.

CHAPTER 9: EVEN THOUGH THE CROPS FAIL

How do you handle disappointment? There have been times when I trusted the Lord for something and it didn't happen, at least not in the way I thought it would. Then I am left in a unique spot where I have to sort through my emotions and feelings. I have built a solid foundation within myself of knowing that He is good and He is the provider despite what my circumstances say. But it doesn't lessen the feelings or emotions that it can bring.

During the first month of my sabbatical I was short $300 on my rent and was feeling very foolish for not working. "This is exactly why I would rather go to work, Lord! This makes me feel so irresponsible and I refuse to be put in an awkward position with my roommates. You have to come through." The closer the day was to the end of the month, the more anxiety I felt. In a moment of panic, I did what I swore I would never do, I withdrew cash from a credit card. I felt so much guilt and shame that I was hearing God's voice wrong. I also felt like I was going against my conviction—not living in debt. I never wanted to go back through paying off $10,000 of debt again. I wrestled through this choice and was still unsure what God was doing.

The next day I got the money I needed for rent but I also

had another bill due and needed food. I kept thinking *if I had just waited, I would've had enough for rent.* Everything else would've worked out. I had to learn to trust in God, even down to the final minute. His timeline is not our timeline and He is not confined by it.

Now, before I make a decision where I'm unsure how to spend money, I simply ask and wait for God's response. For example, I would say, "God, what do you say about this bill? What are you doing in this situation?" In any relationship or in marriage you would talk over these matters with your spouse. God wants access to every part of our lives. Money is so much more manageable when we invite Him into it. God cares about every detail of our lives, therefore He will surely speak to us about our finances.

For me, I hear God best with a "knowing." I either feel peace on something or I don't. When it comes to financial decisions I talk to Him and ask questions about how to handle certain decisions and choices and move forward based on feeling peace or not. The times that I pushed past not feeling peace were the times that I ended up in a mess. I began to learn how to trust the Holy Spirit inside of me and that God cares about every detail.

The Old Testament prophet Habakkuk found the gold to every circumstance, which is our source of joy—rejoicing even though everything around him looked barren. Habakkuk 3:17-19 (NLT) reads, "Even though the fig trees have no blossoms, and there are no grapes on the vines; even though the olive crop fails, and the fields lie empty and barren; even though the flocks die in the fields, and the cattle barns are empty, yet I will rejoice in the Lord! I will be joyful in the God of my salvation! The Sovereign Lord is my strength! He makes me as surefooted as a deer, able to tread upon the heights."

Even though everything around you may look like lack and it may seem God is not coming through, you have a truth you can hold onto. Our truth is that no matter what circumstance we face our joy can stay consistent, never changing, and never wavering. Habakkuk had the choice to look at the lack or to look at the one who provides.

He states, "Yet, I WILL rejoice in the Lord! I WILL be joyful in the God of my salvation (emphasis added)." This is powerful language because it shows the choice that the prophet is making to rejoice and be filled with joy because of who God is. When we can remain joyful and hopeful despite our circumstances we are living as true citizens of Heaven. We are seated in heavenly places; therefore we have access to the Father, who has everything we need. He is our source, not our circumstances.

Some people try to minimize their current reality or pain by using phrases like: "It could be worse." Sometimes you need to acknowledge the pain and the reality that this is actually the worst. Don't brush your pain or frustration under the rug; deal with it. God is big enough to deal with your pain, hurts, and disappointments. Matthew 6:30 (NLT) speaks of God's care for us, "And if God cares so wonderfully for wildflowers that are here today and thrown into the fire tomorrow, he will certainly care for you. Why do you have so little faith?"

Give yourself permission to deal with feelings, but don't allow your feelings to rule you. Even if you are angry with God, you can be real with Him and express your anger. Maybe you need to get real with the Lord today and tell Him how you feel. He knows our every thought anyway, so why not have an honest conversation with Him

When you are giving advice to other people, it's very important not to disregard someone else's feelings by using phrases like: "Oh, it could be worse," or "This isn't that bad; you just need to pray more." The best thing to do is acknowledge the person's pain and feelings but point them to the source of hope, which is Jesus Christ. Ultimately, you can be real with the Lord and let out how you are feeling, cry it out if you need to, but the goal is coming back to the place of knowing that He is good and working all things together for the good. You can have hopeless moments but always come back to a place filled with hope.

This takes time and practice and the only way to learn and grow in this area is by going through times when "the crops fail". When we are sitting in lack and we don't see a way out, when we are in over our heads in debt, when the bills pile up, the doctor's phone calls come, the bad news comes, this is when you have a choice to make. Will you meditate on His Word? Or will you meditate on your circumstances? Paul says in Philippians 2:12-13 (NLT), "We are to work hard to show the results of your salvation, obeying God with deep reverence and fear. For God is working in you, giving you the desire and the power to do what pleases Him."

We are on a journey with the Lord and sometimes you have to walk through tough times in order to grow. We often need a little resistance to push through and lay hold of whatever it is we believe for. Just like with building muscle, the muscle won't build if there isn't resistance.

DISAPPOINTMENTS

It wasn't the first time, probably more like the twentieth time; I stood up in church again because we were going after healing. One of the pastors said, "Tonight we are believing that those who have stood up for healing several times in the past and have not been healed, will get their healing tonight." Faith stirred in my heart as I thought: *this is it; my eye is going to be healed tonight.* A group of people circled around to pray for me. I looked in the mirror to check my eye—it was still the same. I felt my heart wanting to sink because I had once again mustered up the faith that maybe this was the day I would be fully healed.

A few weeks later someone from stage had a word of knowledge that there was someone who had been having issues with their left eye and God was going to heal it today. I felt the same stirring in my heart that maybe today was the day I would be healed. Again, a crowd gathered around me and started praying for my eye. I whipped out my phone to check my eye and it was still the same. I felt disappointed and confused. How many times would I have to keep raising my hand for prayer, and keep coming forward, and keep contending for my miracle?

As I watched many others around me be healed and share their testimonies I had a choice in that moment. I could have sat in the disappointment that God didn't heal me or I could celebrate with those who got healed and continue believing He is the healer. I decided to celebrate with those who were healed and not give into disappointment.

Once I left the service I got into my car and simply said, "God, I don't understand. You called out my sickness and I know you want to heal it and yet I am not healed. I know this is easy for you. If you can cause the lame to walk and the blind to see what is pushing an eyeball back into the socket so that my eyelid will close? I have seen you heal people before so I know you can do it." I didn't devalue the fact that I had set my hope in being healed that night and I talked to God about it. What I didn't do was allow disappointment to cloud my vision of who God is. Naturally, I have a more resilient personality where I will keep getting up even if I have been knocked down multiple times. It is in those defining moments that we have a choice to make whether we will partner with disappointment or process the hurt. We have to be able to get back into a place of truth and not be clouded with disillusionment about who our Heavenly Father is.

My eye didn't heal in that moment but from that day forward I never had any more pain or swelling behind my eyes. The healing process was slow and it has been two years since this happened but my eye has significantly healed and is almost 100% back to normal. I will continue to stand up for healing, even if it's 100 times. I will continue to celebrate other's healing. I will continue to pray for the sick.

Being resilient is an ingredient to longevity. I am thanking Him for my healing as if I am already healed. Today I pray that whatever ailment you have, you will see it healed 100%. I pray that the impossibilities in your body would bow to the name of Jesus and that you would see your full healing.

As believers, we are called to be filled with hope and faith and to believe for the impossible. You carry the DNA of Heaven, which is being filled with expectancy and the assurance that God will come through. Disappointments often come from expecting God to come through a certain way or by a certain time and then it doesn't happen. When a situation doesn't turn out the way we had hoped that it would, we can come to God and process that with Him.

When disappointments come I often remind myself of Isaiah 55:8-9 (NLT), "'My thoughts are nothing like your thoughts', says the Lord. 'And my ways are far beyond anything you could imagine. For just as the heavens are higher than the earth, so are my ways higher than your ways and my thoughts higher than your thoughts'." I don't see the whole picture but He does. God is never absent from your struggle. He is always for you and not against you. In our small minded thinking we can't always see what He is doing but He is always at work behind the scenes, even when it doesn't appear that anything has changed. The pain of disappointment is always an invitation to an encounter with God.

Disappointment is something that we all have to learn how to navigate. What matters is what we do with disappointment. Do you let it change your view of God or do you stand firm on what the Word says despite your experience? If the enemy can keep us disappointed and offended by God he has won the battle. That way the enemy can wedge a separation between your heart and the Father.

Once you get into the mindset of disappointment and allow the wedge to be formed between you and seeking God, you get bitter, pulling away yourself from Him, and seeking comfort in other things. You lose expectation and assume if it has always been a certain way, it will always remain that way. All the while, God is waiting with His arms stretched wide, ready to comfort you and fill you. He wants to meet you in your disappointment. You must take it to God and share with Him how it makes you feel and give Him your pain. In that place He will draw near to you and walk you through your disappointments.

Jesus went through every kind of disappointment a person could go through. "Yet it was our weaknesses he carried; it was our sorrows that weighed him down" (Isaiah 53:4 NLT). Jesus took all of your pain and it was nailed to the cross with Him that day on the mount. He also lost loved ones, was rejected, abandoned by His friends in His greatest time of need, criticized, beat, and eventually crucified. While He was in His greatest time of need, the night before He was crucified, all of His friends could not stay awake and pray with Him.

Put yourself in His shoes. You are hiding out in a garden knowing what was going to take place the next day—your death. Sweat and blood are pouring out of your body and you ask God if there's another way to do this. You ask your friends, please stay awake with me and pray! They all fall asleep. You ask them again to pray and they fall asleep again. There you sit, alone, looking up at the moon and stars, just you and your Father, knowing what tomorrow holds. Just as Hebrews 4:15 (NLT) states: "For we do not have a high priest who is unable to empathize with our weaknesses, but we have one who has been tempted in every way, just as we are—yet he did not sin."

There is no disappointment too great that Jesus cannot empathize and comfort you in. Invite Him into your disappointments and you will find comfort. Your disappointments will be turned into great joy and hope because God will use everything, even the most painful of situations and cause them to work out for the good.

DELAYS

Many times disappointment sets in because of what we perceive to be a delay. During a season of waiting, I came across these two stories in the Bible. Moses was leading the Israelites to the Promised Land and was meeting God face to face on the mountain. The Israelites remained below the mountain waiting on Moses when they became impatient.

"When the people realized that Moses was taking forever in coming down off the mountain, they rallied around Aaron and said, 'Do something. Make gods for us who will lead us. That Moses, the man who got us out of Egypt-who knows what's happened to him?'" (Exodus 32:1 The Passion Translation).

Do you see what happened here? The Israelites were waiting on Moses' leadership but when he took longer than they expected they decided to turn to other gods to lead them. They were on the way to their Promised Land and felt like it was taking too long, so they took matters into their own hands. Think about this. Moses was on the mountain writing the Ten Commandments with God that the Israelites would bring into their Promised Land, when the people become impatient. They had no idea what Moses was doing. How often are we like that? We don't know what God is doing or we think He is taking too long so we take matters into our own hands. All the while, God is at work behind the scenes.

The second story that was highlighted to me is in Matthew 25:1-5. In this parable Jesus talks about God's Kingdom and the ten young virgins who were waiting for the bridegroom. Five of them had enough oil supply to get them through the delay, while the other five did not have enough.

"The smart virgins took jars of oil to feed their lamps. The bridegroom didn't show up when they expected him, and they all fell asleep" (Matthew 25:5 The Passion Translation). In the middle of the night they are awakened to find the bridegroom had arrived but only half of them were prepared to actually greet the bridegroom, while the other five had to run off and get more oil. The virgins who did not use their oil, but waited patiently not knowing when the bridegroom would come were the ones who got to enjoy the banquet feast with him. Even in the delay, do not become impatient and miss the bridegroom or take matters into your own hands.

The first story of Moses speaks about expectations in timing and what God is doing behind the scenes. That if we expect God to come through in a certain time frame and He doesn't, will we also turn aside to modern day idols? Will we turn to Netflix, food, relationships, work, drinking, culture, smoking, porn, shopping etc. to comfort ourselves and fill the void or will we press into more of Him? The point is it doesn't matter what idol you are placing in as a substitute; it is placing an idol where God wants to be your leader. Are you allowing your idol to lead you?

The second story speaks more of being prepared for the delay. This story I believe is speaking more about being filled with the Holy Spirit. Whenever I read about oil in the Bible, I always think of the Holy Spirit. Again, this is an illustration of remaining filled even through the dry seasons of life where it seems that there is a delay in seeing your promises come forth.

Say this prayer with me:

Lord,

May I be found faithful. Please guard me from turning to any idols during this time. Let me not make a way for myself but allow you to lead me and make a way. I know you are at work. Any day is a good day to be surprised by your goodness. You are leading me to take over land. I am on my journey to my Promised Land. Let me not turn to idols or depart from the path you have marked for me. Even in uncertainty and lack of clarity, let me be found faithful. I will enter my Promised Land and I will take over the land you are giving me.

Amen

DEADLINES

If I have learned anything with deadlines, it's that God's timing is not ours. He will honor a deadline, but He is not constrained by them. In our human thinking, deadlines can be overwhelming at times. I also love that God loves to bless us despite how we are acting. I have seen that things tend to move with an ease when I posture myself with hope, expectancy, and faith but I have also seen God come through when I had a bad attitude, was lacking faith, and ready to give up. He knows how to build your faith and at exactly what time He needs to come through.

One day during my first year of ministry school I was ready to throw in the towel and buy a plane ticket to Guatemala and return to the mission field. I didn't understand why my finances were not coming through and I was ready to give up. I even had someone write me a check and said, "You can decide what you want to do with it. I will make it out to you. Whether you use it to pay your tuition or to buy a plane ticket back to Guatemala."

Several days later I was in school and one of the pastors was sharing a testimony where someone had received $1,000. He said he had seen this testimony multiply several times over. I reluctantly raised my hands to receive the testimony for myself but with very little faith that anything would actually happen. I remember thinking I'd be surprised if I actually received $1,000. I was at a pivotal point and had a deadline to pay my tuition within the next coming days. I was getting weary of not having money in this season and having to fundraise for tuition. I believed a lie that God provided better for me on the mission field than He would when I was living in the United States. I had told my pastor I was going to leave school and she told me to give it the weekend and then we would talk on Monday. Sure enough that day the $1,000 testimony was released, I went home to check the mail and there were two $500 checks in the mail. I knew exactly what I was supposed to use it for, my tuition.

Clearly God had called me to ministry school and He

provided yet again. I was brought to tears and overwhelmed at the fact that God had provided this miracle for me. I had the worst attitude that day and was getting really frustrated with the Lord. I was even more humbled that He did this despite my frustration and heart posture. That also broke the lie that I had to be or act a certain way for God to do something for me. All performance was broken off that day after I realized that God truly is a good Father and He doesn't withhold things from me despite how I act.

I had small faith that day but like the lunch with the fish and bread loaf of the little boy brought to Jesus, He was able to multiply it. I once heard a speaker say, "Don't come to God with your nothing. Come to God with your little something and watch Him multiply it."

You never know when your breakthrough is coming. Maybe you are sitting in a large amount of debt and suddenly all of that could change. You could get a backdated check in the mail, a settlement, a rebate, a return, or someone could hand you exactly what you need. Everything can change so suddenly. Suddenly you could be healed. Suddenly, you could be married. Suddenly, you could be out of debt. God is a God of suddenly!

CIRCUMSTANCES

You can tell how mature you are in the Lord by the way you react to your circumstances. Circumstances can be used as a buffer to round off our rough edges and bring us into more complete wholeness. Circumstances apply pressure to reveal what is inside of your heart. It also reveals what your belief systems are. Have you ever noticed you feel at peace when things are going well and you have a lot of money in the bank?

But once the money in your account dwindles down do you remain at peace or are you living in fear and anxiety? The answer to this question will show you where you are putting your faith.

If you answered yes to the question above, don't feel guilty or ashamed. Look at this as an opportunity for growth. Now you have diagnosed a problem and from there you can take steps to grow and change your mindset in this area. Circumstances should not tell us how to behave but rather we should tell our circumstances how big our God is. It requires the same amount of energy to put your faith in God as it does to put your faith in your fears and anxieties. You can declare all day who God is from head knowledge but circumstances will reveal what you truly believe about Him in your heart.

I love the saying, "This too shall pass." When circumstances are not idle, I like to fix my mind on the fact that this will not last forever and this too shall pass. Right now I may be experiencing an illness or empty bank account, but that will not be my forever. Jesus modeled what it was like to have perfect peace despite a raging storm (circumstance) going on around Him. He even did the most offensive thing to the disciples in that moment. He took a nap. I can only imagine their faces as they looked at each other. Is He serious? The waves are raging and crashing against the boat, the rain is blowing sideways, another wave comes and the disciples think this one is going to capsize the boat. "Jesus! Wake up!" Jesus completely calm gets up and rebuked the storm and then turns to ask them, "Why do you have so little faith?"

What about the circumstance you are facing right now? Are you feeling like one of the disciples being tossed to and from within the boat scared that you're going to drown to death? Are you screaming, "Jesus wake up!" What is He saying about your situation? Does it scare Him?

Don't breeze through these questions but take the time to ask yourself and ponder each one. Ask the Father what He is doing right now with this circumstance. What is He teaching you through this? What does He want you to learn? Instead of asking Him "why" questions start asking Him "what" questions. The Holy Spirit loves to answer "what" questions and will counsel you and give you the tools to learn what God wants to teach you.

You may be thinking, *but I can't ignore my circumstance. If you only knew how I felt and what is going on in my life.* This is the tension of living with a hope-filled perspective while walking through tough circumstances. On this side of Heaven there is tragedy, loss, sickness, death and sadness. The reality is that these things do happen but our response to pain, sickness, death, and sadness is where faith kicks in (John 16:33). In the natural there is limited possibilities but in the supernatural there is no limitation.

CHAPTER 10: WHO CARES WHAT YOUR LIFE LOOKS LIKE

I heard the Lord say it so clearly it made me laugh, He said, "Who cares what your life looks like." Isn't that the challenge? It can be so easy to compare our lives to others or be concerned about what friends and family will think or say about our lives, or what culture and society tell us we should be doing. If we dare to swim upstream against the cultural norms, what will be said of us? I have addressed this earlier but this is another layer in the quest of peeling the onion.

TRANSITION

Transition is a normal part of life and no one is immune to it. We all go through many transitions and seasons in life. Whether it be getting married, starting a new job, losing a job, moving, community changes, church changes, leadership changes, having children, starting or ending school, health issues, etc, everyone experiences transition in some way or another. Transition is not a bad thing because if everything always stayed the same, we would never grow or experience all that God has for us. Oftentimes, transition is also marked with periods of waiting before the next thing comes about. Here are four keys I learned during my latest period of transition:

1. Take authority over your day from the moment you get up. Instead of dwelling on what may not have happened yesterday, or looking at what you don't have, declare, focus, and believe in what God could do today. This has to happen from the moment your brain is awake, sometimes even before your eyes open. The enemy tries to slip in before we are even alert enough to realize what we are thinking about.

2. Know that your identity doesn't waiver because of your circumstances. Your identity is not dependent on your car, job, title, what you're doing, or status. Your identity is in being a son or daughter of God.

3. Take one day at a time. Stay in the moment and do not try to figure everything out. In transitions you may not know what decisions to make and that's ok. There are seasons where there is a grace to not plan or make long term commitments but to take things one day at a time.

4. Meditate on the truth and His promises. You have to keep training your mind to think the right thoughts. This doesn't come naturally, so pay more attention to what you're thinking about.

I HAVE BEEN HERE BEFORE

In any season of life we are learning new areas of our minds that need to be renewed. This is why you may find yourself in a similar place that you were in years before. You may think: *Didn't I already learn this? Or I thought I was already past that.* God is so kind to work with our thought lives layer by layer. If He peeled the whole onion at once, it may be more than we could handle. You may feel like you're in the same place you were before but you're not. You are growing and moving forward. This time could be the final layer you are peeling off.

During these times of transition and waiting Paul gives us the strategy to have hope. "Keep your thoughts continually fixed on what is authentic, real, honorable, admirable, beautiful, respectful, pure, and holy, merciful, and kind" (Philippians 4:8 The Passion Translation). Just like Paul had to train himself, we also have to train our brains how to think in alignment with the Kingdom. We have to take every thought captive and make it obedient to Christ. How do we overcome and have victory in this? This victory of a transformed life is in the power of our minds, through what we are partnering our thoughts with and through *learning* to be content.

Paul "learned to be satisfied [content] and undisturbed [peace of mind] in any circumstance. I know what it means to lack and I know what it means to experience overwhelming abundance. For I am trained in the secret of overcoming all things. Christ's explosive power infuses me to conquer every difficulty" (Philippians 4:12 The Passion Translation, emphasis added).

I love this definition of trained. Think of your thought life as you read this definition from *dictionary.com* (source #17): "Teach a particular skill through practice and instruction, over a period of time. Cause to be sharp, discerning, or developed as a result of instruction or practice. Cause (a plant) to grow in a particular direction into a required shape." Over time you are teaching your mind the correct Kingdom thinking patterns. Through instruction and practice you are growing your discernment and causing your thinking pattern to become more and more aligned with the Kingdom.

IN THE WAITING ROOM

As we wait for our promises and dreams to come forth we must establish correct thinking patterns, it sets us up for where we are going. I have seen through waiting seasons in my life some pretty crappy thinking patterns. What comes out of my heart during these trying seasons is more of a problem than the actual waiting time. God uses the "waiting room" to flush out things in us that can't stay for where He is taking us. He wants to get us into a place where no circumstance will sway us.

The dreams and destinies God wants to bring forth in your life cannot be done in your strength. It can come only by way of the Spirit. "'It is not by might nor power, but by my Spirit', says the Lord of Heaven's Armies" (Zechariah 4:6 NIV). How beautiful is it to see someone who has faithfully waited on God to promote them and has not strived to get there. When you strive to get yourself into your dreams and destinies you have to strive to keep yourself there. That sounds exhausting to me. God's promises are meant to be a pure gift. "This is why the fulfillment of God's promise depends entirely on trusting God and his way, and then simply embracing him and what he does. God's promise arrives as a pure gift" (Romans 4:16 The Message Translation). Let's be a people who wait on the Lord with hope, that He will bring forth our destinies and dreams in due season. No matter how long it takes or how contrary your circumstances may look, God is able and mighty to keep His word.

Abraham is our father of promise and his faith was written in the Bible for our benefit, that we too may believe God to do the impossible despite what we are seeing in our circumstances. "He *plunged* into the promise and came up strong, *ready for God*, sure that God *would* make good on what he had said" (Romans 4:20-21 The Message Translation [italics added]). I absolutely love this; he plunged into the promise, fully in, submerged, not doubting or wavering.

"When everything was hopeless, Abraham believed anyway, deciding to live not on the basis of what he saw he couldn't do but on what God said he would do" (Romans 4:18 The Message Translation). Even when your circumstances look hopeless, or those around you say it can't happen, or you are staring at impossibility; you can still have hope. Your hope is in whom God is and what He said He would do.

No matter where you are today, I want to encourage you. You are doing a great job, God is proud of you, and He is relentless and won't ever give up on you. You are a warrior and are more capable than you even realize. If God is calling you to something that looks very odd to the rest of the world, rest assured, because the heroes of our faith were all called to something that looked odd to the world. Let God do the work He needs to do in you so that you will be ready for where He is taking you. Who cares what your life looks like because you only answer to an audience of One.

May you take these verses and be encouraged as you wait, hope, and expect. "Indeed, none of those who [expectantly] wait for You will be ashamed" (Psalm 25:3 The Amplified Bible). "This hope will not lead to disappointment" (Romans 5:5 New Living Translation). Your suddenly is on its way.

UNLEASHING YOUR ADVENTURE

There is an adventure that is waiting to be unleashed inside of you. It's the adventure into the vast unknown. The adventure to say *yes* to Jesus and to whenever and wherever

He wants to take you. There are wild dreams and desires that you have to do the impossible. It doesn't matter if you feel called to change and lead nations, or to raising up the next generation of world changers within your own household, start a business, or go into Hollywood. The adventure waits. It knocks at the door and waits for you to answer.

Martin Luther King Jr., Mother Teresa, Peter, Paul, David, Harriet Tubman and Joan of Arc all had one thing in common. They said *yes* to Jesus no matter what the cost would be. They saw an area they wanted to change, and they devoted their whole lives to that area of influence. They knew that being acknowledged by their Heavenly Father was worth far more than staying comfortable because of the opinions of others.

These heroes of our faith said *yes* to standing on their convictions while they glared death and persecution in the face. They knew it was greater to open the door to the great adventure than it was to leave the door tightly sealed and locked; never opening the door to what was awaiting them on the other side. You can look at any person in history who had a positive impact on society and see that they all went through trials, tribulations, persecution, being misunderstood, and looking crazy but they didn't give up. Keep moving forward— don't give up.

Be willing to stand on the Word of the Lord. Even if it takes years and it doesn't make sense to your natural mind, stand. All God asks us to do is believe. Believe that God is who He says He is. Believe that every word He has spoken will come forth and bear fruit. Everything from Him is good. Every good gift comes from Him. We need faith for what we haven't seen yet. Faith is the substance that gives us hope for our promises and desires. Write out your promises somewhere you can see them and read over them frequently. Remind yourself of where you're going.

Don't kill your dreams. Don't say it's not time. Don't say you are not this or that, or you are not ready. God is with you! You can do anything! He has plans and purposes that He dreamt for you before you were ever formed in your mother's womb. You are called to do the impossible. Adventure beckons. All of creation is longing and groaning for you to walk in the fullness of who God created you to be (Romans 8:22).

Real faith kicks in when we don't have to have everything planned out and understood. Adventures aren't adventures when everything is perfectly planned out and calculated. The Lord honors planning, and there is an extent where planning is good, but we also have to give Him room to do whatever He pleases. If we keep our lives so tightly boxed and contained that He can't move in our lives, then we will never see the great adventure that is inside of us. But if we step out in faith with an attitude of, "God, I know you will come through," that is when we see miracles.

I've heard this quoted often by several pastors but I am unsure of who said it: "Everyone wants to see a miracle but not everyone wants to put himself or herself in the place to need a miracle." Look at the Bible; it is filled entirely with stories of God doing the impossible. In Hebrews 11, the "hall of faith" is filled with people who put themselves in a place where they needed a miracle. Had they not stepped forward and believed for a miracle to come to pass, they may not have been counted as those who had great faith. Even Sarah, who laughed at God in disbelief, came around to have faith that God would actually do what He had promised and He counted her faithful.

Will this generation be a people set apart for the Lord's promises and plans? Will we say *yes* to Him no matter the cost? Will we give Him everything and lay down our lives and be used for Him?

We are reminded of the way God sees us as we lay down our lives to follow him in Proverbs 31:29 (The Passion Translation), "These valiant and noble ones represent the church of previous generations who remained faithful in their pursuit of Jesus. But this final generation will be the bridal company of the lovers of God who do mighty exploits and miracles on earth."

We are that generation. The generation who is so madly in love with God that we only do what He is doing and we go where He is going. We are those who will do mighty exploits that will take us into all of the sectors of society. Miracles, signs, and wonders will follow us as we walk into our divine assignment.

God longs to take you on adventures that will amaze you. You will see new sides of His face and character that you did not know before. Each of us was created to impact the world in a different way, yet collectively together as the body of Christ. No one else can do what God has called you to do. Lay down all distractions and all noise and follow Him. Jesus didn't come for us to follow a religion, or a system, or a bunch of principles. He came so that we would follow Him.

It is time to take courage and rise to the call that you have been commissioned to bring Heaven to earth (Matthew 6:10). You have a unique destiny that only you can fulfill. Dress yourself in the armor of God, and use the promises that have been spoken over your life to wage war against the darkness that opposes your destiny.

I encourage you with Ephesians 6:10-17 (NIV italics added): "Finally, be strong in the Lord and in his mighty power. [11] Put on the *full armor* of God, so that you can take your stand against the devil's schemes. [12] For our struggle is not against flesh and blood, but against the rulers, against the authorities, against the powers of this dark world and against the spiritual forces of evil in the heavenly realms. [13] Therefore put on the full armor of God, so that when the day of evil comes, you may be able to *stand your ground, and after you have done everything, to stand.* [14] *Stand firm then,* with the belt of truth buckled around your waist, with the breastplate of righteousness in place, [15] and with your feet fitted with the readiness that comes from the Gospel of peace. [16] In addition to all this, take up the shield of faith, with which you can extinguish all the flaming arrows of the evil one. [17] Take the helmet of salvation and the sword of the Spirit, which is the word of God."

Today will you say *yes* to the next step? It doesn't have to be the whole picture; you may not know that part yet. God is responsible for the how; we are responsible for our *yes.*

DECLARATIONS

- I say *yes* to Jesus and His leadership in my life.
- I trust that God's plans for me are good.
- I can take big risks because God will never leave me.
- I have a unique destiny that only I can fulfill.
- Today is the day the Lord has made and I will rejoice and be glad in it.
- I have all that I need and I will not go into debt.
- I am generous and freely give to others.
- I am well liked and people enjoy being around me.
- I am bold, confident, and free to be me.
- I agree with the words spoken over my life and will be everything God created me to be.
- Today is a great day for good things to happen to me.
- Those who trust in the Lord will NOT be put to shame.
- I am walking through my open doors and opportunities are coming to me.
- My lost family members are coming home to the Lord.
- I will give birth to every dream that has been put inside me.

Father,

Your love for us is so unfathomable, we will spend our entire existence searching out and seeking to know the depths of your love. Set a desire and hunger within our souls that will only be quenched by you. You stir up our passions, desires, and giftings. You are so well pleased with us whether we are doing or simply being. I pray that the very words of this book become a platform for others to jump into the abyss of your deep love and to radically say yes to the adventure You have in store for them.

Amen

NOTES

Introduction:

1. King, Martin Luther, Jr. "I Have A Dream..." I Have A Dream... Accessed January 01, 2018. https://www.archives.gov/files/press/exhibits/dream-speech.pdf.

2. "Faith." English Oxford Living Dictionaries. Accessed January 12, 2016. https://en.oxforddictionaries.com/definition/faith.

3. Engle, Lou. "God had a dream and wrapped your body around it." Twitter. September 08, 2014. Accessed January 20, 2018. https://twitter.com/louengle/status/509075017695756289?lang=en.

Chapter 3: Process

4. "Sozo." Blue Letter Bible. Accessed January 22, 2018. https://www.blueletterbible.org/lang/lexicon/lexicon.cfm?t=kjv&strongs=g4982.

5. "What Is Shemittah? The Sabbatical Year basics: absolution of loans, desisting from all field work, and the spiritual objective of all the above." Shemittah. Accessed January 22, 2018. http://www.chabad.org/library/article_cdo/aid/562077/jewish/What-Is-Shemittah.htm.

6. Roberts, Frances J. *Come Away My Beloved.* Classic ed. Uhrichsville, Ohio: Barbour Publishing, Inc., 1970.

7. Bevere, John & Lisa. "How God Grows Us Up-Part 1." July 17, 2017. Accessed July 17, 2017. https://itunes.apple.com/us/podcast/conversations-with-john-lisa-bevere/id218453800?mt=2.

8. *Snow White and the Huntsman.* Directed by Rupert Sanders. Performed by Kristen Stewart, Chris Hemsworth and Charlize Theron. Australia: Universal, 2012. Film.

9. Gunter, Sylvia, and Arthur Burk. *Blessing your spirit: with the blessings of your father and the names of God.* Birmingham, AL: The Fathers Business, 2005.

10. GotQuestions.org. "What is the Logos?" GotQuestions.org. January 04, 2017. Accessed February 02, 2017. http://www.gotquestions.org/what-is-the-Logos.html.

Chapter 4: Transforming Your Mind
11. Staik, Athena, Ph.D. "The Neuroscience of Changing Toxic Thinking Patterns (2 of 2)." Psych Central.com. December 29, 2013. Accessed August 17, 2016. http://blogs.psychcentral.com/relationships/2011/08/the-neuroscience-of-changing-toxic-thinking-patterns-2-of-2/.

12. JB Cachila. Wed 7 Dec 2016 6:39 GMT. "3 Signs of Poverty Mentality." Christian News on Christian Today. December 07, 2016. Accessed January 3, 2018. https://www.christiantoday.com/article/3-signs-of-poverty-

mentality/102738.htm.

Chapter 5: Saying Yes to Jesus

13. "O.T. Names of God." Blue Letter Bible. November 1995. Accessed August 19, 2017. https://www.blueletterbible.org/study/misc/name_god.cfm.

14. Sorge, Bob. *Secrets of the Secret Place.* Grandview, Missouri: Oasis House, 2001.

Chapter 6: Courage But Not The Absence of Fear

15. Brother Andrew, John L. Sherrill, and Elizabeth Sherrill. *God's Smuggler.* Minneapolis, MN: Chosen, 2015.

Chapter 8: Breakthrough

16. Brother Andrew, John L. Sherrill, and Elizabeth Sherrill. *God's Smuggler.* Minneapolis, MN: Chosen, 2015.

Chapter 10: Who Cares What Your Life Looks Like

17. "Trained." Dictionary.com. Accessed September 21, 2017. http://www.dictionary.com/browse/trained?s=t.

23695123R00095

Made in the USA
Columbia, SC
11 August 2018